Mary Mulari

Appliques

with *Style*

Lynda—
Happy applique!
Mary Mulari 10-7-00

Published by

krause
publications

700 E. State Street • Iola, WI 54990-0001
Telephone: 715/445-2214

Please call or write for our free catalog of publications.
Our toll-free number to place an order or obtain a free catalog is 800-258-0929
or please use our regular business telephone 715-445-2214
for editorial comment and further information.

Book design by Stacy Bloch
Cover and color section design by Jan Wojtech
Photography by G.W. Tucker Studio
Illustrations by Mary Mulari

Mulari, Mary
Mary Mulari Appliques with Style
1. Applique   2. Sewing   3. Title

Library of Congress Catalog Number: 98-85566
ISBN: 0-87341-683-X

Printed in the United States of America

*This book is dedicated to honor
the memories and lives of two extraordinary women:
my mother, Helmi Koski and my friend, Margaret Croswell.*

Acknowledgments

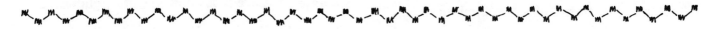

This is about sharing.

It is a pleasure to prepare this list of people and companies I appreciate for all their help with this book. So many people have been willing to share their knowledge, products, and views of the sewing marketplace. This makes a huge difference for me—and for you as a reader—in what I include in this book.

Seven sewing machine companies and their educators and support staffs have provided machines, expert advice, and stitching samples: BabyLock, Bernina, Elna, New Home, Pfaff, Singer, and Viking.

Other companies provided products and information and a person and phone number to call with questions: Aleene's, Birch Street Clothing Co., Duncan, Fiskars, In Cahoots, June Tailor, Kunin Felt, LJ Enterprises, P&B Textiles, Pellon, Sulky of America, Therm

O Web, The Warm Co., and Wimpole Street Creations.

And then there are my sewing world friends and teachers who are always ready to share their knowledge and words of cheer: Nancy Bednar, Gail Brown, Anita Covert, Rita Farro, Donna Fenske, Barbara Gash, Sue Hausmann, Carol Heidenreich, Jane Hill, Jasmine Hubble, Janet O'Brien, Barb Prihoda, Jill Repp, Linda Teufel, Faith Wilde, and Nancy Zieman.

In my daily life in Aurora, Minnesota, I have the support and inspiration of family, friends, and my morning walking group. They are always willing to share their good humor and ask about the progress of my book.

So my acknowledgments are a recognition of those who have shared with me. Now I share with you. It's a circle, and I hope you'll keep it going by sharing your knowledge and ideas with someone new to sewing.

Table of Contents

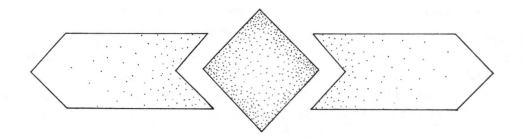

Introduction

I'd like to welcome you to a new world of machine applique, a world very different and much larger than it was even ten years ago.

A historical study of applique reveals this technique in some form in nearly all countries and cultures around the world. Applique is the process of sewing one piece of fabric to another for the purpose of ornamentation. It is decorative sewing, a "painting" technique you and I use as sewing artists. We can use this technique on garments and accessories we buy or make.

The purpose of this book is to share fresh as well as traditional applique methods and materials and to present another collection of designs. You may remember my self-published book, *Applique Design Collection*. When copies of that book ran out, it was time to write a new version with different and contemporary designs. Thanks to the encouragement of Nancy Zieman and my husband Barry, both of whom said I need to do this book, you are holding it in your hands.

Be sure to check out all the chapters and sections on applique enhancements, "Found Art," and the Celebration Squares button-on movable applique system. I hope you'll see that applique has limitless potential.

And please don't limit yourself to sewing in your use of the design section. From letters and comments, I know my readers have used my applique designs for cake decorating, bulletin board decorations, outlines for embroidery patterns, sign lettering, and much more.

To make this book easier to use, take it to a print shop for a spiral binding. The cost is minimal and the spiral binding will keep the book open flat while you are using it.

You may have noticed that the word "applique" in this book does not have the traditional accent on the final e (appliqué). Through my experience and years of use of this word and technique, I have chosen to drop the accent.

The introduction—the part you probably read first—is the part I write last. As I prepared all the chapters, instructions, and designs, I discovered the recurring themes and key words of this book: practice and experiment. They'll show up in every chapter because they are such important steps in your creation of applique that looks professional.

Now let's get started.

Mary Mulari

The dictionary definition of applique: A decoration or trimming made of one material attached by sewing, gluing, etc. to another.

Chapter 1

Applique Material

This is a list of "consumables" because these products are used up and you need to replenish your supply. Products are listed here by brand name, and I suggest that you try all of them. For experimentation, start with one-half to one yard and when you've found your favorite products, buy a minimum of three yards. Then you'll be prepared for late night applique binges when the sewing stores are closed.

Fusibles and Adhesives

This category covers the products that securely attach applique fabrics to a background fabric so stitching around the edges can be accomplished without tucks or puckers in the fabric. Remember the days before these products were invented and all we had were common pins? It's amazing that anyone could achieve a smooth stitching line.

Paper-backed fusible web is what the name suggests: a paper sheet with fusing material added to one side. By using this product, you can make applique shapes with a fusible backing, similar to an iron-on patch for mending.

Wonder-Under® by Pellon was the first of these products, so many stitchers refer to any of the products by that name. (It's like Kleenex® and all the other facial tissues that followed.) In my opinion, paper-backed fusible webs have revolutionized applique.

It is important to follow the instructions given with each of the paper-backed fusible webs because iron temperatures and steps vary. It is possible to "over bake" fusibles if your iron is too hot, which will make it difficult to maintain smooth surfaces on the designs, especially after laundering. Also pay attention to the water temperature suggestions for laundering the finished appliques.

Products in this category include Aleene's Hot Stitch Fusible Web (both Regular and Ultra Hold), Heat 'n Bond (Lite for sewing and Regular), Steam-A-Seam™ 1 and 2, and Wonder-Under (Regular and Heavy Duty). Always use the product recommended for sewing to avoid stitching problems with your sewing machine. The heavy duty varieties can gum up your needle.

Here are general instructions for using paper-backed fusible webs:

1. Cut a piece of paper-backed fusible web slightly larger than the applique design. Place the fusible side of the product down over the applique pattern and trace around the design on the paper side. Trace all parts of the design separately (Fig. 1). You will find this a rough surface for tracing, so draw slowly for accurate tracing. Remember that the design will be reversed when it's cut from fabric, so letters, numbers, and all designs with a definite right and left side should be traced backwards. In this book, all designs are presented backwards so tracing can be done in one step with paper-backed fusible web.

Fig. 1

2. Place a piece of applique fabric slightly larger than the piece of paper-backed fusible web right side down on the pressing surface. Then place the fusible side of the traced design on the wrong side of the applique fabric. Following manufacturer's directions for temperature and length of time to hold the iron down, fuse the paper to the fabric (Fig. 2). Be patient and hold the iron down with firm pressure. If the design piece is large, lift up the iron, move it to another area of the design, press and hold the iron in place, and repeat until the entire design is fused. (When you fuse with the iron, press and hold it rather than moving it back and

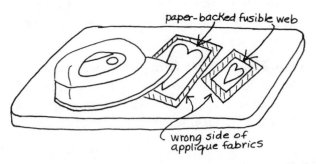

paper-backed fusible web

wrong side of applique fabrics

Fig. 2

forth across the fabric as you do when ironing clothing.) Wait a few seconds for the paper to cool before you pick it up.

3. The next step is to cut the shape out of the fabric, following the pattern drawn on the back of the fabric. To ensure that the paper will pull away easily from the back of the fabric after cutting out the design, start the separation process in one corner of the paper and pull it away from the fabric slightly into the pattern area (Fig. 3). This will guarantee that there is one free edge

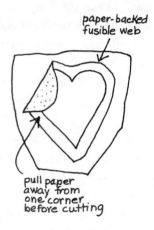

paper-backed fusible web

pull paper away from one corner before cutting

Fig. 3

to grab onto after cutting out the pattern. This is especially important for applique fabrics that fray. If it is difficult to remove the paper backing from the edge of the design, the applique edge may become frayed as you work to separate the layers of paper and fabric. On non-fray fabrics such as Ultrasuede®, the fabric edges are strong, so if you have problems separating the layers, tear the paper layer by twisting the edge. Discard the paper backing after removing it from the back of the fabric shape.

4. Position the applique shape on the background fabric. On a woman's garment, plan the design location by following the recommendations on page 47. Following the manufacturer's directions, fuse the design to the background by pressing and holding the iron on all areas of the fabric applique. Some fabrics, such as Ultrasuede and lamé, must be protected by a press cloth. Place the cloth over the designs before fusing.

If you question whether or not to use a press cloth for fusing, you'll be safer to use one or test a piece of the questionable fabric in advance. Securing the applique to the surface to which it will be sewn is one of the keys to successful and professional looking applique.

Other variations of paper-backed fusible webs are Steam-A-Seam 2 by the Warm Co. and AppliqEase™ by HTC. These fusible products both produce applique shapes with a fusible and tacky back surface. This surface will allow you to temporarily stick design shapes to fabric and other surfaces and then reposition them with no pinning required. When you have determined the placement of the design shapes, fuse the shapes in place with the iron following the manufacturer's directions. Test in advance with fabric scraps.

The backing of AppliqEase provides support for thin or hard to manage applique fabrics and also makes see-through light colored fabrics less sheer when placed on darker background fabrics.

Steam-A-Seam 2 has a layer of release paper on each side of the fusible product. Trace designs on the side with the web still attached to it; the other layer will separate from the fusing first, providing the tacky surface for temporary positioning of the appliques.

Fusible web without paper backing. Three products fit this category: Stitch Witchery®, Fine Fuse™, and Sol-U-Web™. To fuse an applique with any of these brands, you must plan to place the fusing material between two layers of fabric (the applique and its background) or between the applique and an applique (or Teflon) pressing sheet (see the equipment list and description in the following chapter).

When using an applique pressing sheet, place the fusible product directly on the sheet with the applique fabric (slightly larger than the fusible piece) right side up (Fig. 4). Fuse by pressing the iron down firmly on

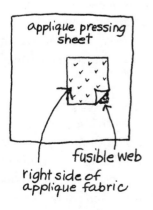

applique pressing sheet

fusible web

right side of applique fabric

Fig. 4

the fabric. Wait a few seconds before peeling the fabric off the pressing sheet. The back of the fabric will be shiny from the melted fusible. Cut the design from the treated fabric and fuse it to the background.

Experiment with these products and a variety of fabrics. Many applique stitchers prefer the soft feel of appliques constructed with these fusibles. Remember that Sol-U-Web is a temporary fusible only—you must follow up with stitching to make sure the applique won't separate from its background after laundering.

To avoid getting pieces of the fusible stuck on the iron, be sure to discard or move scraps away from the ironing surface.

Adhesives

Glue stick. The name describes the product: a stick of soft glue in a tube. This product offers a temporary hold for appliques. Use a glue stick made especially for fabrics rather than one for paper only.

Rub the glue stick on the back of an applique, rubbing from the center to the edges to prevent distorting the fabric (Fig. 5). Position and finger press the treated applique to the background and sew into place.

wrong side of fabric

Fig. 5

Test this product and its use before relying on it for a larger applique shape or design. You may find that it holds the applique shape in place as you sew, but if it moves while you are stitching, add a few pins to secure the shape better. (My recommendation: several short applique pins, as described in the following equipment chapter.)

My favorite use of the glue stick is for applique enhancements such as rickrack or narrow braid. Rub the glue stick on the back of the trim, working on an applique pressing sheet that can be cleaned or a surface that can be discarded, such as a sheet of paper from your recycling bin. Position and pat the glued trim on the fabric and you'll be able to sew it on without using pins.

Liquid Pins. This bottle of liquid is a temporary adhesive for holding two fabrics together. It dissolves when the fabrics are washed.

Liqui-Fuse™ Apply fusing liquid where you want it with this bottle of liquid fusible web. The liquid is applied to the wrong side of the applique. Once the applique is ironed, the fusing is permanent and no sewing is required.

Fusible spray. Spray adhesives (Sulky KK 2000 and ATP-505®) offer a temporary fusible surface for appliques. They are easy to use, odorless, and the sprays do not harm the environment. Read the instructions on the spray cans to check the manufacturer's instructions.

On a throw-away surface such as newspaper, place the applique or other fabric surface wrong side up. Spray from 6"-10" away. The bonding is temporary and will disappear in two to five days. It also makes the applique shape repositionable. The sprays can also be used to temporarily hold stabilizers in place on the back of background fabric.

Fusible thread. These 100% nylon fusible threads (ThreadFuse and Stitch'nFuse by Coats) are heavy white threads that melt when pressed with an iron. Use the fusible thread in the bobbin. Straight stitch around an applique shape, with the fusible thread in the bobbin so it comes out on the wrong side of the fabric. Press the applique in place and the fusible thread will melt to hold the shape to the fabric so it can be satin stitched around the edges (Fig. 6). The use of this thread eliminates fusible web on appliques, for a softer feel. It also can be used in the lower looper of the serger, as described in Serger Appliques on page 30.

satin stitching over fusible thread stitching line

Fig. 6

Interfacing

Occasionally interfacing can improve appliques by strengthening and stabilizing the fabric from which they are cut. White or light colored fabrics can benefit from interfacing to make them less sheer on dark backgrounds.

To avoid producing thickness and bulk in an applique design, use lightweight interfacing. My preference is tricot knit fusible interfacing which is soft and lightweight. Fuse the interfacing to the wrong side of the applique fabric, a piece larger than the applique design. Then cut the applique shape from the interfaced fabric (Fig. 7).

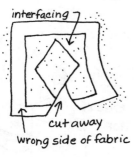

interfacing

cut away
wrong side of fabric

Fig. 7

The same interfacing can also be used to stabilize the wrong side of the background fabric beneath the applique area if extra support is needed.

Thread

In years past, the only thread used for applique was standard sewing thread. While it is still acceptable, there are now many other choices that can enhance the appearance of appliques.

The first rule is that any thread used for machine applique must be of good quality and new. Don't even think about using the thread you inherited from your mother or grandmother. Also skip the thread displays offering ten spools for a dollar (Fig. 8).

Ten
Spools
$1.00

Fig. 8

If you use standard sewing thread for applique, these threads will be all cotton or poly/cotton blends. Depending on the stitch you select, standard sewing threads generally work well and in many stitch patterns, such as the blanket stitch, they will not be prominent. For satin stitching, many experts recommend all cotton threads and even more specifically, all cotton machine embroidery threads.

Once again, experiment with thread possibilities, colors, stitches, and needles to make the best choices for each project and your sewing machine.

For the bobbin, use quality sewing thread in a color to match the top thread (tension problems will not be visible)

or use special bobbin thread such as the white and black Sulky Bobbin threads or Madeira Bobbinfil.

Clear nylon thread is a great choice for invisible applique stitching. It is now finer and softer and easier to work with than clear thread used to be. Another variation is "smoke" shaded nylon thread which blends well with darker fabrics. For applique, this thread is usually used as the top thread only, with standard or bobbin thread in the bobbin.

Rayon thread adds luster and a special attraction to appliques, especially in a solid stitch like the satin stitch. Forty (40) weight thread is commonly used for applique stitching, although some sewing artists prefer 30 weight, which is heavier. The array of colors available in rayon threads is amazing and extensive. Variegated and twisted colors are also available for more applique options.

Metallic threads offer another appealing edge finish for appliques. To eliminate thread breakage, use a machine embroidery needle and sew slowly. Many sewing artists find that a line of Sewer's Aid, a non-staining liquid silicone, applied to the spool of thread will smooth the thread passage through the machine (Fig. 9). Loosening the machine's top tension may also help when sewing with metallic threads.

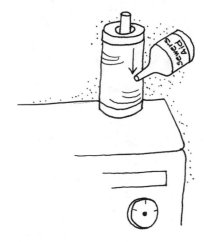

Fig. 9

Thread colors are an important consideration. They contribute significant detail to appliques. For subtle edges on appliques, select thread to closely match the applique fabric. (This is also my recommendation for beginners in machine applique because stitch glitches are not so obvious.) For a more noticeable edge finish, select thread to contrast with the fabric. Metallic and rayon threads add an additional shine while clear nylon thread adds almost no sign of stitching. On elegant fabrics like lamé and Ultrasuede, extra stitch detail may not be necessary. Try out your thread choices on practice fabric scraps and then decide.

Sewing machine needles

Sewing machine needles are also a consumable product since they need to be replaced frequently. The first advice is to always use a new needle for each machine applique project. When you think about it, you'll realize that the needle penetrates the fabric many many times in applique, sometimes more than it would if you were sewing a simple garment. Check your sewing machine manual for recommendations of needle sizes for various fabrics and projects.

For many applique projects, a Universal point needle in a size 80 or 90 will work well. A larger needle (100 or 110) may be needed for thicker threads or metallics. Machine embroidery or metallic thread (Metafil) needles are also available and are good choices for rayon and metallic threads. If you are sewing knit appliques on knit fabrics, you may find a stretch needle to be a good choice and a solution if the machine skips stitches. Specialty needles for special effects in applique are the wing needle and double needles. Experiment with both these needles and a variety of stitches, fabrics, and threads to see the effects you can create.

Fig. 10

One of my favorite uses for the double needle is stitching flower stems (Fig. 10). Select a satin stitch and a double needle in size 2.0mm, 3.0mm, or 4.0mm. Practice first and turn the sewing machine wheel by hand, observing the swing of the double needle and making sure it clears the opening in the presser foot and the opening to the bobbin. Many sewing machines have a double needle safety button to push when using a double needle. This button can save you the agony of breaking a double needle because it regulates the stitch width.

See the bibliography for other books ("Point Well Taken" from In Cahoots) and information about sewing machine needles.

Fray stopping liquids

Fray stopping liquids are used occasionally in applique to prevent raveling of threads or fabrics (Fig. 11). Three of these products are FrayCheck™, No-

Fray, and Aleene's Stop Fraying. They are sold in small bottles and not to be confused with bottles of sewing machine oil. (I've heard some bad stories where this has happened.)

Fig. 11

Tracing paper

Tracing paper comes in a tablet in the art supply store or stationery department and is a valuable addition to your sewing room for applique and other projects. It is a sheer and strong paper, much better to use for tracing than tissue paper. Once you have a tablet on hand, you'll wonder what you did without it. If you need to trace a mirror image of a design, it'll be much easier to do with tracing paper since you can see through it without holding it up to a window or light box. Many of the techniques described in this book require tracing paper.

Stabilizers

Stabilizers have increased in number and variety in recent years. We have many new choices and I suggest that you try them all to best determine your favorites for applique and other sewing projects. Hint: When you purchase several pieces or packages of stabilizers, be sure to label each one before you use or store it. My favorite way to label is to write the stabilizer name along one edge or inside the roll it's sold on (Fig. 12). Then I cut pieces off the stabilizer from the opposite edge. Ideally, you'll also store the stabilizer with its instruction sheet, but if the two get separated, you will be able to match the instructions and product later.

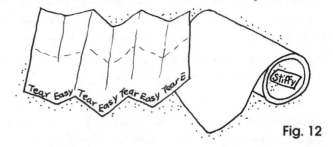

Fig. 12

Stabilizers are essential for producing professional looking appliques and other creative projects. Adding a stabilizer beneath the fabric to be decorated gives the sewing machine's feed dogs a firmer base to work on as the fabric moves under the presser foot. If you try satin stitching on fabric (especially knits) without a stabilizer, you'll produce stitching with a "wavy" surface, not the flat surface you desire.

Tear-away stabilizers are used to add stability and firmness for applique. Pinned, basted, or temporarily spray fused in place on the wrong side of the fabric to be decorated, they provide control and prevent distortion of the background fabric and puckering.

Select the stabilizer weight to match fabric weight. On a medium to heavy fabric, a lightweight stabilizer does not add enough support unless another layer or two is added. On a lightweight fabric, a heavy crisp stabilizer in the back will distort the fabric and stitches when it's torn away.

Pellon Stitch-N-Tear® was the first tear-away stabilizer invented, so many sewing artists call this entire category "stitch and tear." It has a crisp surface and a medium weight. Pin, baste, or spray fuse it to the wrong side of the background fabric, stitch the applique, and then carefully tear it away and discard it or save large sections for stabilizing smaller designs.

Sulky Tear-Easy® is a lightweight soft stabilizer that does what its name suggests—tears away easily after stitching so there's less danger of distorting stitches or fabrics. It can also be used in layers.

Sulky Stiffy® is twice as heavy as Tear-Easy so this crisp and firm tear-away supports heavier fabrics.

Easy-Stitch by HTC is a perforated stabilizer with a slip resistant backing. It tears away easily after applique stitching. Many machine embroiderers prefer it.

HTC RinsAway® is a firm stabilizer that can be torn away or dissolved in water. To avoid distorting stitches, you can cut away the stabilizer close to the sewing lines and then soak it in water to dissolve the rest.

Sulky Totally Stable® is a soft stabilizer with a "waxy" slick side. With a dry iron, press on the paper side to temporarily adhere it to the wrong side of fabric. Stitch, then tear away the stabilizer. This product is preferred by many for knit fabrics to prevent the fabrics from shifting or stretching during sewing. It makes soft fabrics easier to handle.

White or black Swedish Tear-Away Paper from Birch Street Clothing Co. is a soft, lightweight, polyester-based stabilizer on a roll. It tears away cleanly from stitched areas and remains soft inside the stitching so the stitching area remains flat. The black stabi-lizer works well on darker fabrics, as it blends and matches better than white stabilizers.

Household products such as coffee filters, freezer paper, or typing paper can be used in an emergency. I recommend that you use legitimate stabilizer products for best results and manageability.

Mary's Hints for Removing Tear-Away Stabilizers

Because it's easy to be overly enthusiastic about this last step of applique stitching and tear away the stabilizer too vigorously, I recommend the following procedures:

1. If you tear with your right hand, hold the fabric and stabilizer with the side of your left thumb on the stitching line. Tear away from your thumb, but do it carefully and slowly so you won't disturb the stitches (Fig. 13).

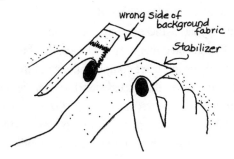

wrong side of background fabric

Stabilizer

Fig. 13

2. If even careful tearing distorts or pulls out the stitches, cut the stabilizer away instead.

3. If you've used more than one layer of stabilizer, tear each layer away separately.

4. Use tweezers to remove stabilizer in small spaces. Use a screwdriver to loosen and work stabilizer edges away from stitching. These tools won't cut into fabric like a seam ripper or scissors. Another helpful tool is a Stanley® staple remover. The rounded smooth tip slides in to grasp the stabilizer and then you can pull up to remove it (Fig. 14).

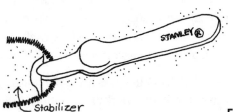

STANLEY®

Stabilizer

Fig. 14

Cut-away stabilizers are often left in place in ready-to-wear garments, or they can be removed by cutting, not tearing. The advantage of using cut-away stabilizers is that there is no possibility of ruining or distorting applique stitches by tearing. These products must be removed by cutting or left in place to support the designs and stitches through wear and laundering. They are also very soft products and do not irritate the skin.

Sulky Cut-Away Soft 'N Sheer® is a lightweight textured stabilizer that works well with lightweight knits and wovens. After pinning it in place and sewing, cut the stabilizer away or leave it in to hold the design stable through laundering and wearing. I have also discovered that it makes a good see-through press cloth.

Sulky Cut-Away Plus® is a mid-weight product, good for use with medium to heavyweight fabrics and thicker than Soft 'N Sheer. It too is pinned or temporarily fused to the wrong side of the background fabric before applique stitching and is cut away after. It has a soft feel and remains that way through handling, but it holds designs and stitching in shape.

Water soluble stabilizers seem like they have magical properties! They are transparent films that can be used beneath or on top of stitching areas. Placed on top of a textured fabric like terry cloth, these stabilizers support machine stitches as they flatten and cover the terry loops. Pin, baste, or spray fuse the stabilizer in place, complete the stitching, and carefully tear or cut away the excess stabilizer before rinsing the fabric to remove all the traces of the stabilizer. It may be necessary to rinse twice or soak the fabric to remove all the residue, especially if more than one layer of this stabilizer is used.

Always consider the fabrics before using water soluble stabilizers. Test to make sure that fabrics can tolerate the water removal process. Many silks, for example, would be ruined by spraying or rinsing in water.

Store these stabilizers in tightly sealed zip-close bags to keep them away from moisture or humidity.

Three water soluble stabilizers are Sulky Solvy (the original weight), Super Solvy (heavier weight), and Avalon by Madeira.

Design Plus from LJ Designs is a paper product that can be layered over and/or under the base fabric. A layer above and below slippery or sheer fabrics can help to control the fabric. This stabilizer can be torn or cut away after stitching and then the remaining stabilizer is sprayed or rinsed to remove it.

Sol-U-Web by Pellon was listed previously as a temporary fusible, but it also works as a stabilizer that dissolves with water after stitching. It is a soft product that can also be layered on top of the fabric to prevent stitches from sinking into thick fabrics like sweatshirt fleece or terry cloth.

Liquid and spray stabilizers are applied to stiffen washable fabrics so additional layers of stabilizer are

Fig. 15

not needed. They are applied wet and the fabrics must be allowed to dry completely before sewing, a process that can be speeded with a hair dryer, fan, or a hot iron and pressing cloth. The stabilizers wash out in laundering or the fabrics can be rinsed out thoroughly two or more times to completely remove the residue. If possible, experiment on fabric scraps to determine the stiffness of the fabric and the number of coats to apply.

Perfect Sew™ is a non-toxic liquid stabilizer with a citrus scent. Once dry on fabric, it makes the fabric stiff enough for heavy embellishment or embroidery. For more control in applying the liquid, squeeze it from the bottle onto a foam rubber painting pad which can be brushed on the fabric (Fig. 15).

When you want to sew satin or decorative stitches directly on fabrics such as t-shirt or sweatshirt knits, mark the stitching lines with a chalk marker. Wet the lines with Perfect Sew and allow to dry. The stitches do not sink into the fabric but lie on top of it so the stitching details show.

Aleene's Stiffen Quik Instant Fabric Stiffening Spray, Sullivan's Fabric Stabilizer, and household spray can be sprayed on in coats so the backround fabric can be made as stiff and stable as necessary. You may want to experiment on a scrap of fabric. After stitching is complete, the spray stabilizer can be washed out with hot water and detergent.

Iron-away stabilizer is a muslin-like fabric that is chemically treated (non-toxic) to be heat sensitive. It is a good choice for delicate fabrics that can tolerate heat from the iron and projects you don't want to wet to remove the stabilizer. Pin or baste the stabilizer on top and/or under the fabric to be appliqued. After stitching, use a hot dry iron to press the stabilizer until it turns brown. Be watchful so you don't scorch the fabrics. Then brush away the powdery residue with an old soft toothbrush. As you experiment with this stabilizer, you may find that it will work with the iron set at a slightly cooler temperature for heat sensitive fabrics or threads. Sulky Heat-Away™ is the stabilizer in this category.

Chapter 2:

Equipment for Applique

I will assume that you have a basic sewing basket full of supplies like rulers, scissors, pins, washable marking pens, chalk markers, and of course, a seam ripper.

To prepare for sewing appliques, assemble these tools.

1. **Applique pressing sheet**, also called a Teflon sheet. This ordinary looking piece of translucent white plastic-like material is a wonderful piece of applique equipment. I often think it should have its own bells and whistles to give it distinction (Fig. 1).

The Wonderful Applique Pressing Sheet

Fig. 1

The sheet is actually heat resistant so you can iron directly on it. It can be used to fuse non-paper-backed fusible webs like Sol-U-Web and Fine Fuse to the wrong side of fabric. This makes the fabric an "iron-on patch"—very slick on the wrong side. Then, all you have to do is cut the applique shape from the treated fabric. I also use the sheet when I want to protect a fabric surface from the iron.

Pay attention to the sheet's surface after using it. If residue from fusibles is left on the sheet, you may mess up another project. (Ask me how I know this!) Keep your pressing sheet clean. You can use a fabric softener dryer sheet to clean it.

Pressing sheets come in various sizes and thicknesses. The professional grade is thicker than the regular grade.

A bonus use: When you're not using the sheet for sewing preparations, consider it as a liner for a cookie sheet. It's an amazing piece of equipment.

2. **Light table** (Fig. 2). While this piece of equipment is not essential, you'll never regret having one. With a light source beneath the table, it is easy to trace designs—much easier than holding books, tracing paper, and pencils up to a window.

Fig. 2

You can make your own light table if you have a glass topped coffee table or a dining table with separating sections (Fig. 3).

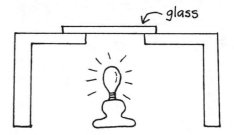

glass

Fig. 3

3. **Rotary cutter** with straight and wavy blades, **mat**, and **ruler** (Fig. 4). Rotary cutters cut fabric fast and accurately. The wavy edge blade cut on a non-fray fabric like Ultrasuede is an interesting edge finish.

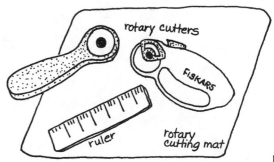

rotary cutters

FISKARS

ruler

rotary cutting mat

Fig. 4

4. Applique scissors (Fig. 5). These uniquely-shaped scissors work well to trim away fabric close to stitching lines and away from other awkward areas. The duck-billed blade slides easily under fabric. I like these scissors because they're sharp all the way to the tips.

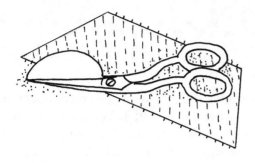

Fig. 5

5. Iron (Fig. 6). Keep this essential piece of equipment near the sewing machine so you use it often. Many steps in applique require an iron for fusing or pressing. Make sure yours is clean on the bottom so you don't press any unwanted residue on a special applique.

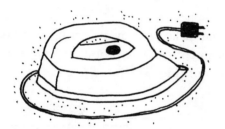

Fig. 6

6. Press cloth (Fig. 7). My favorite press cloth is a thin white cotton cloth I can see through to check on the alignment of applique pieces before I fuse them in place. Anytime I'm not certain the fabrics can withstand the heat or direct imprint of the iron, I use my press cloth over the applique. I recommend this habit to you too.

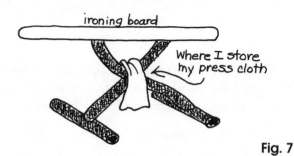

iron ing board

Where I store my press cloth

Fig. 7

7. Applique pins (Fig. 8). The short fine pins are great for pinning an applique in place. Use many of these pins, starting at the center and pinning to the edges. Unlike longer thicker pins, these don't obstruct the presser foot.

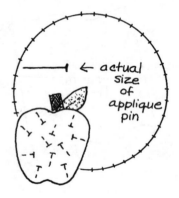

← actual size of applique pin

Fig. 8

Chapter 3:

Fabrics for Applique

It used to be that 100% cotton fabrics in primary colors were the only fabrics used for applique. Now our choices have expanded beyond the traditional ones and we have so many more fabrics to select.

The first consideration for applique fabric is its washability. If you are decorating a washable garment or accessory, it makes sense to add appliques in fabrics that are also washable. If the project will never be laundered, feel free to select dry clean only or non-washable fabrics.

Also consider the fabric's weight—the applique should be cut from fabric lighter in weight than the background to which it will be sewn. As an extreme example, think of how wide wale corduroy appliques on a soft silk blouse would drag down the silk fabric when the blouse is worn.

Prewashing is always a good idea, to test both the applique fabrics and the background. You'll want to know before sewing if fabrics have problems due to color leakage, extreme wrinkling, etc. Many fusible web manufacturers recommend prewashing fabrics to remove fabric sizing, which prevents a good bond between the fusible and the fabric.

The only fabric I do not prewash is Ultrasuede even though it is a washable and dryable fabric. I machine dry prewashed fabrics for just a few minutes to bounce out the wrinkles. Another product to prewash is fusible interfacing. It is best treated by gentle hand washing and hanging to dry to avoid ruining the fusible side.

Here are some fabrics to consider for applique. Check your collection for additional possibilities.

❖ 100% woven cottons
❖ Satin
❖ Chiffon & sheers
❖ Velour
❖ Lamé
❖ Wool
❖ Velvet/velveteen
❖ Quilted fabrics
❖ Lycra
❖ Rayon
❖ Terry cloth
❖ Fur & fake furs
❖ Felt
❖ Suede & leather
❖ Flannel

❖ Linen
❖ Ultrasuede
❖ Taffeta
❖ Polyester
❖ Corduroy
❖ Lace
❖ Nylon
❖ Silk organza
❖ Felted wool
❖ Vinyl
❖ Silk
❖ Mesh
❖ Knits
❖ Polarfleece®
❖ Denim

Add fabric appliques to paper products such as gift bags, scrapbook covers, stationery, and gift wrap. Fuse the designs on with a dry iron and a press cloth over the top of the appliques.

Choosing Fabric Colors for Applique

Some of the designs in this book are labeled with color suggestions and other designs can be made in any color. But what will those colors be?

The color selection part of an applique project can take a lot of time. Gather your fabric possibilities and background fabric and begin combining and eliminating. Pin pieces of fabric to the background and hang or pin the background piece to a bulletin board or wall so you can stand back and see it from a distance. Squint to narrow your vision. Do you see bold colors jumping off the background color or do they blend? Decide on the effect you want to create with your applique. If you can afford the time, leave the fabric swatches on the item to be decorated so you can see it several times during a day or evening. Ask someone else, even a non-sewing member of your household, for opinions. This has worked for me.

For a safe approach, use only solid colors. That way you won't have to worry about clashing prints that distract the eye from the applique design. If you want to include printed fabric, choose one print and coordinate the other fabrics to blend or match the print.

Study appliques and embellishments on ready-made garments and you'll see that the safe approach is often ignored; prints and patterns are surprisingly combined and they are attractive. The more you pay attention to fabric combinations, the more you'll learn about what appeals to you and the colors you like to see together.

One of my favorite ways to create appliques is to use tone-on-tone fabrics so the applique fabrics are the same, or nearly the same, color as the background. For example, on a red knit jacket I chose two shades of red Ultrasuede for leaf appliques. The effect is subtle and classy. Then I blanket stitched the leaf shapes on the jacket with orange rayon thread so there is a bit of edge definition to the designs. Thread colors can blend or contrast, depending on the effect you desire. Experiment with this new approach to applique. It's very different from the bright and colorful cute designs you sew for children.

Whole books and extensive sections in others have been written on colors and color selection. Many quilting books cover this topic also and present ways to sort and combine fabric colors. Just as in a quilt, color selection can be key to an applique's attractiveness.

> Ultrasuede is great applique fabric for adults and children. It is machine washable and dryable, tasteful, and distinctive. For children, Ultrasuede appliques are durable and retain their colors through numerous wearings. Another special feature of this fabric is that blind children and adults can enjoy the feel of Ultrasuede appliques.

Chapter 4:

Assembling & Marking Applique Designs

Some of the applique designs in this book are built of many pieces (Fig. 1). Here's help for putting them together and for transferring and marking details and stitching lines.

Fig. 1

A little bit of planning is a smart idea when assembling multi-piece designs. On the tulip/heart design illustrated, cut the center stem piece 1/4" longer on the top and bottom so it can be inserted beneath both designs (Fig. 2). Cut the side stems with squared off ends, as shown by the dotted lines on the pattern, and place the leaf shapes over the top.

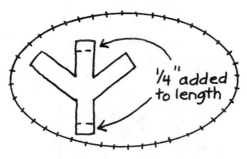

1/4" added to length

Fig. 2

Trace and number all the design pieces separately on paper-backed fusible web (Fig. 3).

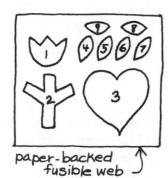

paper-backed fusible web

Fig. 3

Cut the design pieces from the paper, leaving a paper border around each piece (Fig. 4). Then fuse each piece to the wrong side of the fabric chosen for each design. Cut out the shapes and remove the paper backing.

Fig. 4

To assemble the design just as it appears in the book, trace the entire design on tracing paper. Flip over the paper for the mirror image of the design and place an applique pressing sheet over the design. Place and overlap all applique pieces in the correct position (Fig. 5).

applique pressing sheet

Fig. 5

Carefully place the iron over the design to lightly fuse it together so you can move it in one piece to the background fabric where it will be permanently fused and appliqued.

For a design with separated parts and lines, such as the one illustrated, transferring the shape placements and lines to the background fabric is a little more challenging (Fig. 6).

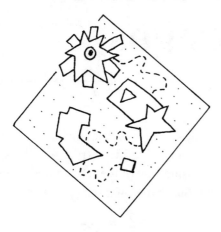

Fig. 6

There are several ways to transfer marks, lines, and shapes to the background fabric. Netting (bridal tulle) offers one transfer medium. Cover the applique design in the book with clear plastic wrap to avoid transferring pen marks to the book, or make a photocopy of the design to trace on. Place a piece of netting over the design. Trace around the design with a water soluble marking pen (Fig. 7).

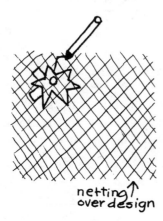

netting over design

Fig. 7

Move the tracing to the fabric background where the design will be located. For some designs, such as the one featured, the netting will be flipped over for the mirror image of the design as it appears in the book. Pin the netting to the fabric (Fig. 8).

Now trace the lines on the fabric with a washable or chalk marker, depending on the fabric color. Remove the netting. As you can see, the netting never becomes part of the design but works well as a transfer method for the design markings.

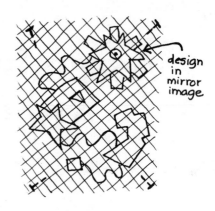

design in mirror image

Fig. 8

Water soluble stabilizer presents another method and variation for transferring designs. Place the semi-transparent stabilizer over the design and trace the lines with a washable marking pen or other fine line marker.

For the design in the illustration, turn over the marked stabilizer and place the tracing against the right side of the fabric background where the designs will be stitched. Slide the applique shapes in position under the tracing. Lift the tracing and fuse the shapes to the background. Then pin the tracing back in place. Straight stitch on the connecting lines of the design and remove the stabilizer or satin stitch along the lines and then remove the stabilizer (Fig. 9). This method works especially well on textured fabrics and prevents the stitches from sinking into the fabric.

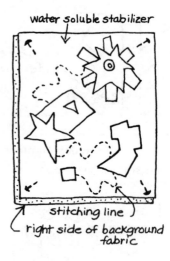

water soluble stabilizer

stitching line
right side of background fabric

Fig. 9

Either method can also be used on the back side of the fabric background for sewing from the reverse. If you choose this approach, place the traced side of the tulle or stabilizer up instead of flipping the traced side over (Fig. 10).

Stabilizer with tracing

wrong side of background fabric

Fig. 10

Don't be afraid to try the free hand method of marking design details. Study the design, then draw your own lines or marks with a chalk or washable marker. You may create something better than what I've drawn! It'll be your distinctive designer touch.

For applique designs you plan to use often, cut them from quilting template plastic or other translucent or clear plastic sheets. Then the edges will be firm and the design can be traced quickly and easily. If the plastic is easy to see through, you can position the pattern over a specific design or area on the fabric.

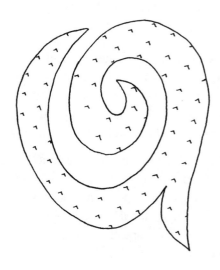

Chapter 5

Preparing Your Sewing Machine for Applique

After assembling the materials and equipment for applique, it's time to get your sewing machine ready. You needn't the newest, most deluxe machine to do applique, but your machine must be in good condition and able to stitch a variable width and length zigzag stitch.

Find the machine instruction manual to assist in your machine checkup. Clean the lint out of the bobbin area and case. Drop in some oil if the manual suggests it. Put on a new needle, spool of thread, and bobbin thread. (Read through the previous chapters of recommended materials and equipment.)

Check your sewing machine manual and find an applique presser foot. It may be called an "open toe" foot or a "special purpose" foot. Your local sewing machine dealer may have additional new presser feet available for applique.

Attach the applique presser foot. It will have an open space in the center. The great advantage of this opening is that you can view the stitching and see ahead to guide the fabric. The foot may be metal or clear plastic. On the underside of the foot there may be a wide groove to allow satin stitching to pass smoothly under the foot without jamming the machine (Fig. 1).

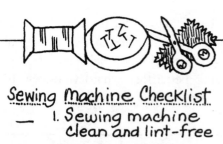

Sewing Machine Checklist
— 1. Sewing machine clean and lint-free
— 2. Applique presser foot attached
— 3. Applique thread
— 4. Full bobbin
— 5. New needle
— 6. Practice fabrics and stabilizer

Fig. 2

Select the machine stitch you plan to use. (Satin stitching information is in the next chapter.) Test the stitch and the machine settings on practice fabrics and on the same stabilizer you'll use on the applique project. Sew a few stitches and stop to check the appearance. You may want to loosen the top tension on the machine. This will keep the bobbin thread from showing on the top side of the applique. Note and record the machine settings for future sewing. Write them in this book or in your machine instruction manual (Fig. 2). I have discovered that it's not a good idea to trust our memories.

Now you're ready to try satin stitching.

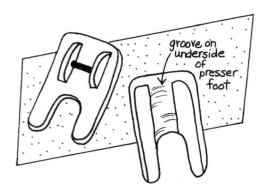

groove on underside of presser foot

Fig. 1

Chapter 6:

The Basics of Satin Stitching

Through my contacts with sewing artists across the country, I hear again and again the same sad tale about the person who has sewn successfully all her life, completing every kind of garment and accessory known to man. Yet when she tries satin stitching for the first time, her stitching is imperfect and far below the professional look she's accustomed to creating at her sewing machine.

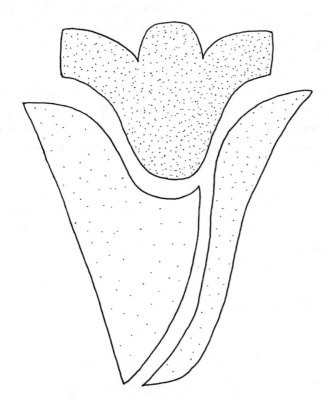

This is normal. Satin stitching is one sewing stitch that requires practice, and what your mother told you about "practice makes perfect" certainly applies here. I like to warn first-time satin stitchers that their first stitching may not please them and that their initial practice work or project may be discarded. I repeat, this is normal and everyone needs to allow themselves to be a beginner.

Prepare your practice piece by fusing the flower design on one end of a white or light-colored background fabric (Fig. 1).

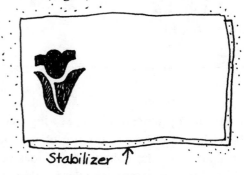

Stabilizer ↑

Fig. 1

This design has the edges, corner, points, and curves that you need to practice. Refer back to the fusibles section in the Materials chapter for information on fusing or adhering an applique design to a background fabric. Don't forget the stabilizer. Have a pen handy for recording stitch notes on the fabric.

Sit at the machine in a comfortable chair and concentrate on relaxing your elbows and shoulders. More of your body will relax then too. This is practice and not a test. It will be fun, so lighten up and don't expect too much of yourself the first time you try (Fig. 2).

Relax

Fig. 2

Adjust the machine to the satin stitch setting, referring to your machine manual for help. Some machines have a preset satin stitch, but on many machines, satin stitching is an adjustment of the zigzag stitch. I compare satin stitching to the solid, close together stitches on one side of a buttonhole, but a bit wider. Use a dark color thread and for the first stitch width setting, use a 2.5mm setting and a stitch length setting of .5mm. On the fabric beside the flower, try the stitch to check its appearance. Write the settings on the fabric near the stitching (Fig. 3).

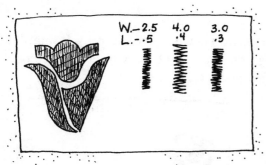

Fig. 3

Loosen the top tension of the sewing machine if the bobbin thread shows on the top of the fabric. In ideal satin stitching, the bobbin thread does not show on the right side of appliques and the top thread should be pulled down to the underside. On some machines, this adjustment to the tension is accomplished by passing the thread through an extension on the bobbin case (Fig. 4).

Fig. 4

Continue to experiment by sewing additional rows of satin stitching with wider and narrower settings. Label the settings of each row. My preference for satin stitching is a narrower rather than a wider stitch. I think it is easier to control and guide the stitching and any imperfections are less noticeable. Thread color that matches the applique fabric will also help to blend the stitching into the edge of the fabric.

When you are ready to begin satin stitching around the practice flower, position the fabric under the press-er foot in the center of an edge. The left swing of the needle goes into the applique fabric and the right swing goes just over the edge of the fabric and into the background fabric (Fig. 5).

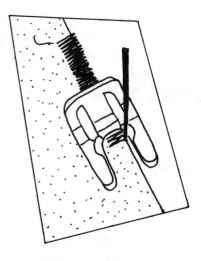

Fig. 5

Stitch slowly at first and set your machine for the "needle-down" position (if it has this feature) so the machine stops sewing with the needle down in the fabric.

Guide the stitching with your hands resting lightly on the fabric, not gripping or pulling it. For gently curved edges, guide and turn the fabric without stopping to pivot the fabric. You may find that a little bit of speed in your sewing will help you sew without having to stop and pivot the fabric.

What's pivoting? On corners, points, and small circles, you will need to stop stitching, preferably with the needle down in the fabric, raise the presser foot, and pivot or turn the fabric slightly. This will allow your next stitches to slightly overlap the previous stitches and create a solid line of stitching without v-shaped gaps (Fig. 6).

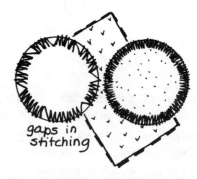

gaps in stitching

Fig. 6

On an inside curve, stop stitching with the needle down and in the left position. On outside curves, stop with the needle down in the right position, lift the presser foot, and pivot the fabric before lowering the presser foot and continuing to stitch (Fig. 7).

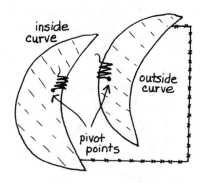

Fig. 7

For a corner, stitch all the way to the point, stopping with the needle down in the right position. Lift the presser foot, pivot the fabric, lower the foot, and resume sewing. The first few stitches will overlap the corner stitches. If the machine wants to jam, stop stitching and move the fabric ahead just a bit to continue the stitching (Fig. 8).

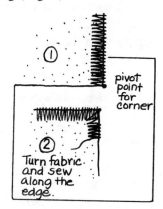

Fig. 8

About points: With a narrow satin stitch and a not-so-sharp point, you can stitch as described above (Fig. 9).

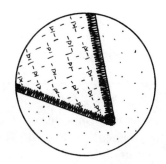

Fig. 9

To achieve a tidy look with a sharp point, stop sewing 1/4" from the tip of the point and narrow the stitch width. Sew to the point, stop and pivot the fabric so you can continue to stitch with the narrowed stitch width about 1/4" up the second side of the point and then ad-

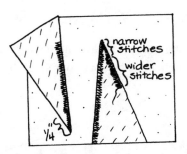

Fig. 10

just the stitch width back to the original width (Fig. 10). It takes practice to become proficient at point applique.

On an inside corner like the two in the flower shape, you may wish to mark the corners with short guide lines to the inside of the shape. Stitch until the needle comes to the line, stopping in the left position (Fig. 11). Pivot the fabric and continue sewing along the next edge. With more practice, you'll be able to sew without marking the guide lines.

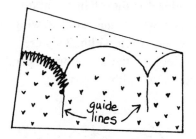

Fig. 11

Sew around each shape and overlap three or four stitches where you meet the beginning stitches. Stop, cut the threads, and pull the top threads back to the wrong side of the fabric. Tie knots or secure the threads with a dot of FrayCheck before cutting off the thread tails. Remove the stabilizer. (See the hints for tear-away stabilizer removal on page 11. Press the design on both the top and bottom.

What if you don't like the stitching and want to remove it and try again? With sharp embroidery scissors, cut through the center of the applique stitching on the right side of the fabric (Fig. 12). Pull the thread ends out from the wrong side. This leaves a neat and clean finish on the right side of your work. Check the condition of the stabilizer before you restitch, and if necessary, add another piece under the area to be satin stitched again.

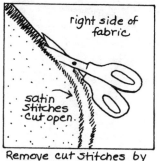

Remove cut stitches by pulling out from the wrong side of fabric. **Fig. 12**

Satin Stitch Variations

Many sewing machines have interesting variations on a plain satin stitch, so check out your stitch list (Fig. 13).

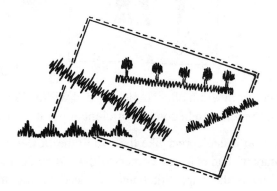

Fig. 13

Another idea for the plain satin stitch is to begin stitching at one width, and after sewing a short distance, change the stitch width. This creates a wavy or choppy edge look to the stitching, depending on how much you vary the width (Fig. 14).

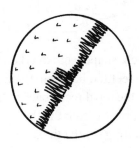

Fig. 14

Satin Stitch Extensions

There's nothing wrong with satin stitching all by itself, but the addition of another row of stitching builds a more distinctive applique framework. Here are some stitch combinations to try, and these are just the beginning.

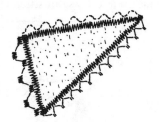

Fig. 15

Bar tack applique with satin stitching. This unique use of the satin stitch was shared by Barb Prihoda, machine embroiderer extraordinaire!

1. Fuse the applique shape to the fabric background. Straight stitch around the shape very close to the edge (Fig. 16).

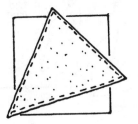

Fig. 16

2. Set the machine for a medium to wide satin stitch (I used a 4.0mm width).

3. Sew four to five stitches over the edge of the applique and the straight stitching line, stopping the needle in the right position and down in the fabric. Raise the presser foot and pivot the fabric 180 degrees so the stitching you just completed is to the right of the needle (Fig. 17). Sew four to five stitches again, stopping with the needle in the left position.

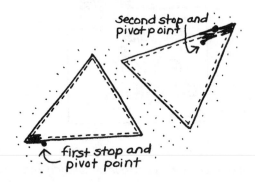

second stop and pivot point

first stop and pivot point

Fig. 17

4. Stitch around the design shape with these satin stitched bar tacks. The applique has an unusual edge with this stitch variation.

> A hint for sewing appliques on ready-made clothing: Fuse on the applique, add the stabilizer, and turn the garment inside out. This step will place all the excess fabric, sleeves, etc. above the stitching area where it is easier to watch and keep away from the stitching area.

Chapter 7:

Applique Variations

There's more to life than satin stitching! The world of applique has expanded with new methods. No longer do we have to make all appliques flat, in cotton fabrics, satin stitched, and cute. Take time to try these intriguing techniques to create appliques with artistic style and dimension.

Blanket Stitch Applique

You may know this method as invisible applique or buttonhole applique. It uses the blanket/buttonhole stitch found on most sewing machines (Fig. 1). But this single stitch in combination with different threads offers many options for applique. It can be either visible or invisible.

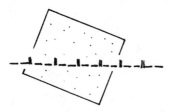

Fig. 1

The invisible version is produced with clear nylon thread or a thread color that matches the applique fabric exactly. The straight stitch portion is next to the applique edge and the horizontal stitch into the applique (the bite) is adjusted to be very narrow (Fig. 2).

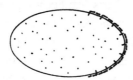

Fig. 2

Visible blanket stitching is sewn with contrasting color thread or with the direction of the stitch turned out. These visible effects can imitate the look of hand stitching as a bold accent around an applique. Black thread is often chosen as a contrasting color for all the shapes in one design; on a black background, black stitching brings the base fabric color into the design. You can also make this stitch highly visible by sewing the horizontal (bite) portion of the stitch extending into

the background fabric (Fig. 3). Many sewing machines make this stitch easy to flip with a mirror image button.

Fig. 3

Another way to add density and visibility to the stitch is to use two threads and a size 100 needle to accommodate them. Try stitching on practice fabric first.

Straight Stitch and Scrub Cover Applique

For this stitch variation, use only the straight stitch and the reverse button on your machine. This variation allows you to do applique stitching on even the most basic machine.

Now that we have expanded our applique fabric possibilities to include more than woven cotton fabrics that ravel, choose a non-fray fabric, fuse it to a background fabric, and straight stitch around the edges (Fig. 4). Matching or clear nylon threads hide the stitching and a contrasting thread color will add a narrow line of detail around the edge.

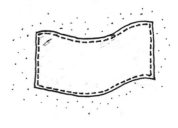

Fig. 4

A more casual and novel use of straight stitching is the scrub cover applique stitch (Fig. 5). Fuse an applique to a background, then stabilize the back of the fabric. Sew forward and backward through the design, pivoting the fabric so the stitches are directed to cover all areas of the design. Stitch over the edges or stop at the edge before you reverse the straight stitching. Just stop sewing whenever you feel like it. This couldn't be easier or more fun!

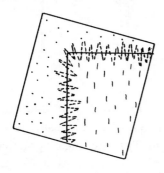

Fig. 5

A scrub stitch variation is stitching randomly back and forth over applique edges only, as illustrated (Fig. 6).

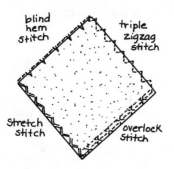

Fig. 6

Decorative Stitch Applique

Here's where the world of applique stitching opens up with endless possibilities. How many decorative stitches are available on your machine? Most all of them can be used creatively as applique stitches—when you're open-minded!

Many machines have a collection of stitches called "utility" stitches which are designed for everyday sewing tasks. Examples include the blind hem stitch, triple zigzag, overlocking edge stitches, and stretch stitches (Fig. 7).

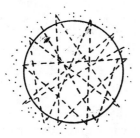

Fig. 7

These and all the others can be used to produce uncommon applique stitches. Challenge yourself to use and develop ordinary stitches for applique. Once again, experiment. Try different threads and vary the stitch length and width (Fig. 8). Write notes on your discoveries and save your practice fabrics.

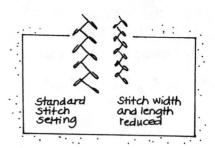

Fig. 8

Beyond utility stitches are many more choices. Test them also. Some stitches may appear too wide, but altering both width and length may adapt them for applique stitching. Also consider using a double needle or wing needle for an entirely different appearance. Extend the stitches beyond the edges of appliques to change the outline of a design (Fig. 9).

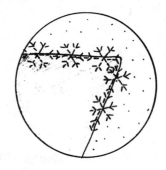

Fig. 9

Echo Applique

The inspiration for this applique variation came from a t-shirt I found in Paris. An additional row of decorative stitching is sewn on the background fabric around the applique shape. This extra stitching adds a frame and builds out the design (Fig. 10). Plan for extra space around design shapes so the extra stitching can be added.

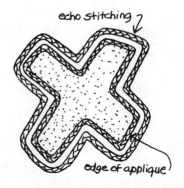

Fig. 10

1. Select a decorative stitch for sewing around the applique and then use the same stitch 1/4" from the edge of the applique. On a knit fabric like a t-shirt or sweatshirt, the application of a liquid stabilizer such as Perfect Sew will prevent the stitches on the knit from sinking into the knit.

2. Apply the liquid after stitching on the applique, allow it to dry, and then stitch the "echo" row.

Lined Applique

The advantage to lining appliques is that there are no raw edges to worry about. This presents many options for securing appliques, since the edges do not have to be sewn down.

My first lining fabric choice is netting or tulle. It adds almost no bulk or thickness to appliques and it's inexpensive and easy to find and use. It's available in colors so you may want to have both dark and light netting for different projects. I have discovered other lining fabrics which I will describe following the instructions for lined applique.

1. Trace an applique design on the right side of the fabric. Cut a piece of netting slightly larger than the applique and place and pin it over the traced design (Fig. 11).

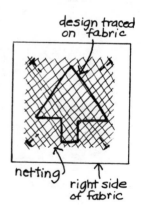

design traced on fabric

netting

right side of fabric

Fig. 11

2. Adjust the machine stitch length to 2.0 and sew around the applique along the traced line. Trim and clip the seam allowances to about 1/8" or trim with a pinking shears (Fig. 12).

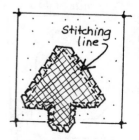

Stitching line

Fig. 12

3. Press the applique from the fabric side. Carefully cut a slash in the center of the netting only and pull the fabric through the opening (Fig. 13).

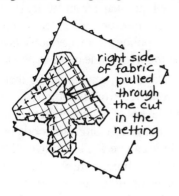

right side of fabric pulled through the cut in the netting

Fig. 13

4. Finger press the edges of the applique and insert a small crochet hook into the opening to push out and smooth the seam edge. Press the applique flat.

5. Attach the applique to background fabric in any number of ways: blanket stitching around the edge, sewing a spiral line from the edge of the shape to the center, securing the shape with a button sewn in the center, or any method of your choice (Fig. 14).

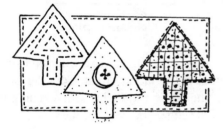

Fig. 14

Other lightweight lining fabrics I've discovered are Soft 'N Sheer cut-away stabilizer and Sol-U-Web. Soft 'N Sheer is not as transparent as netting, so you may prefer to trace the applique shape on it instead of on the right side of the applique fabric.

Sol-U-Web lines the applique and then serves as a fusible to hold the applique to the background fabric. Cut a small slash in the Sol-U-Web lining and pull the fabric through the opening very carefully (it's not as strong as netting). After finger pressing the seam edges out and using the crochet hook, place the design on the background and press. The design is now temporarily fused in place and must be sewn around the edges for a permanent hold.

Liberated Applique

Sometimes it's fun to make an applique that isn't traditionally attached to its background. With this method, the applique edges are sewn first on a stabilizer, the stabilizer is removed, and the applique is free (liberated!) to be attached to a garment or accessory in a variety of ways.

1. Cut the applique shape from fabric. For a more substantial applique, fuse two pieces of cotton fabric together and cut the applique from the double layer, or fuse interfacing on the wrong side of the applique fabric.

2. Select a stabilizer, remembering that it will be torn away or removed from the stitched edges of the applique. Two layers of water soluble stabilizer or a single layer of a heavier version are good possibilities, since the applique can be wet to remove all traces of the stabilizer. Other choices are Swedish Tear-Away stabilizers made of polyester which tears away cleanly from stitching. Pin or use spray fusible to hold the applique shape on the stabilizer (Fig. 15).

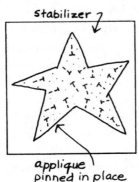

Fig. 15

3. Stitch around the edges. Use a satin stitch or satin stitch variation if the fabric ravels. Consider other stitches too; if the fabric frays a bit with stitching that covers less of the edge, you may like the look (Fig. 16).

Fig. 16

4. Remove the stabilizer. Press the applique. Attach it to a hat, a purse, a sweatshirt—you choose! Sew only in the center to secure the design, straight stitch close to the stitching already on the edge, hold it in place with a shank button pinned on top of the applique, or use both a button and stitching (Fig. 17).

Fig. 17

Dimensional Applique

Breaking away from the old rules of applique, we can construct designs that are not flat or attached to a background on all sides. Here is an easy example of a design that adds the feature of depth and dimension to applique decorations.

Octagon Layered Flower. Each flower is made up of two lined octagons, the top shape smaller than the bottom one.

1. Cut four pieces of fabric slightly larger than the octagon patterns. Make two sets with two pieces of fabric right sides together (Fig. 18).

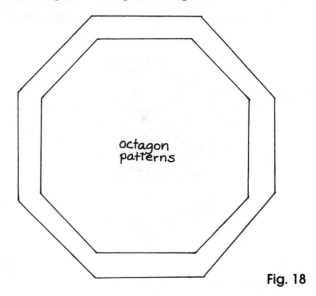

octagon patterns

Fig. 18

2. Trace the outline of each octagon on the wrong side of the top piece of one set of fabrics (Fig. 19).

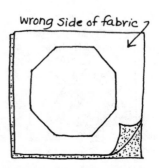

wrong side of fabric

Fig. 19

3. Sew around the octagon shapes on the tracing lines, then trim and clip the seam allowances. Use a pinking shears to trim and clip in one step. Cut a small slash opening through one side of each lined shape and turn the fabrics right side out (Fig. 20).

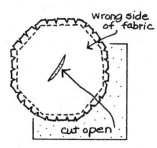

Fig. 20

4. Finger press the seam edges and then press each shape flat. Make a fold in the center of each shape as illustrated (Fig. 21).

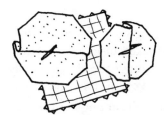

Fig. 21

5. Place the smaller folded octagon on top of the other with slashed sides meeting. Pin and sew through the centers to attach the two layers together.

6. Add a ribbon, button, pom pom, or other trim in the center of each flower. Pin or sew the flowers to trim a bag, hat, or any surface that needs a dimensional applique. Cut leaves using the pattern below. Make a fold in the leaf end to give dimension to the leaf.

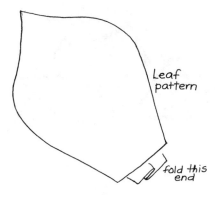

Reverse Applique

This technique is the opposite of regular machine applique in that the decorative fabric is placed on the wrong side of the fabric background. After some stitching to secure the two fabrics together, the right side of the background fabric is cut open to reveal the decorative applique fabric beneath.

This version of reverse applique uses the argyle or diamond shape in different ways to show the possibilities with a simple design and easy stitching and cutting (Fig. 22).

Fig. 22

Select the background fabric, keeping in mind that the wrong side of the fabric shows on many of the diamonds. Also decide whether you want a fray or non-fray fabric. The effects will vary because the cut fabric edges are not covered by stitching. Denim is an interesting choice because the wrong side of the fabric is a different color than the right side and the fraying adds distinctive texture to the edges.

1. Trace the diamond shapes on paper and cut them out. Trace the shapes on the background fabric in the arrangement you want. Remember that the tracing line will be the stitching line (Fig. 23).

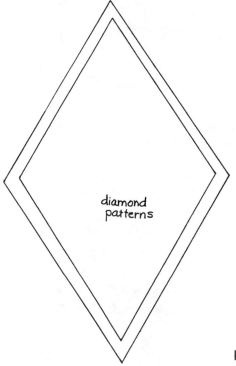

Fig. 23

2. Cut decorative fabric for the wrong side of the design area. You can use one large piece for the entire arrangement or cut pieces of fabric larger than the diamond shapes for each individual diamond. To stabilize and strengthen the decorative fabric, fuse lightweight interfacing to the wrong side of the fabric.

3. Pin the decorative back fabric to the wrong side of the background fabric with the right side up (Fig. 24). Sew around each diamond shape with a short-length (2.0) straight stitch.

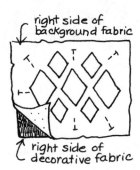

right side of background fabric

right side of decorative fabric

Fig. 24

4. Cut open the diamonds to form the pattern you want. Cut close to the seam. On the diamonds with a portion of the fabric folded back, it's important to cut very carefully to keep a neat edge to fold back (Fig. 25).

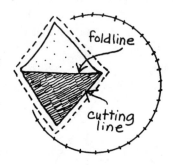

foldline

cutting line

Fig. 25

5. Fuse and sew down the loose corners and edges of the diamonds (Fig. 26).

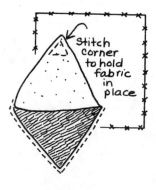

Stitch corner to hold fabric in place

Fig. 26

Overlay Applique

This is one of the easiest applique variations. The designs are traced from printed fabric, duplicated in another fabric, and sewed on top of or near the original design.

1. Here's another project that will be much easier to complete with tracing paper. (See Materials on page 10.) Through the tracing paper, you'll be able to see and quickly trace a design from the fabric (Fig. 27).

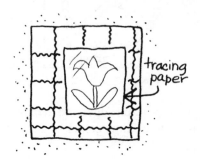

tracing paper

Fig. 27

2. Turn the tracing over so you can trace it backwards onto paper-backed fusible web. Then fuse the traced shape to the wrong side of the overlay fabric and cut out the shape. Peel off the paper backing.

3. Place and fuse the applique over the design, next to it, or in another position. Place stabilizer on the wrong side of the printed fabric and stitch the overlay in place.

Serger Applique

Serge simple geometric shapes (no circles!) to create novel applique shapes with edge detail. Straight lines and gentle curves work best for serging (Fig. 28).

Fig. 28

1. Select a three or four thread stitch or a rolled edge on the serger. Use fusible thread in the lower looper. This will later allow you to fuse the designs in position on a garment or accessory.

2. If using woven cotton fabrics for the appliques, fuse lightweight interfacing on the back of the fabric.

3. Cut triangles, squares, rectangles, or shapes from fabric, cutting them slightly larger than you want them to appear. The serger will trim off a bit of each edge. Consider the geometric designs on page 50 or the woven design on page 57 and 78.

4. Serge the edges, leaving thread tails on the ends if you wish. To eliminate the thread tails, trim them to 1/2" and then fuse them to the wrong side of the designs when placing the designs in position on the background fabric (Fig. 29).

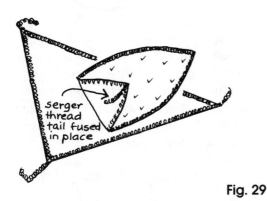

Fig. 29

5. Plan the design arrangement and fuse the designs to the background, tucking in or leaving the thread tails exposed. Follow up by stitching either a straight or narrow zigzag stitch to permanently attach the shapes to the fabric. Match the sewing thread to the serger thread so the stitching is hidden.

Padded Applique

Add a puffy surface to an applique for a different look. There are several ways to do this.

HTC Fusible Fleece™ can be fused to the wrong side of appliques before they are sewn to the background fabric.

1. Cut the fusible fleece 1/4" smaller than the design all around (Fig. 30). I recommend cutting the fleece with a pinking shears so the puffy edge is not as noticeable as a line through the applique after it is sewn in place. For thinner padding, separate and pull away the top layer of the fleece.

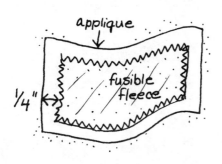

Fig. 30

2. Following the manufacturer's instructions, place the fleece fusible side up and then the applique over it, wrong side down (Fig. 31). Cover with a press cloth and press lightly for 10-12 seconds. Remember that the harder you press, the more you reduce the loft or puffiness of the fleece.

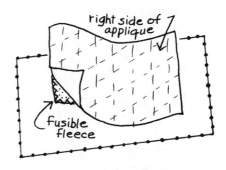

Fig. 31

3. To secure the padded applique to the background fabric, spray the back of the applique with fusible spray or use pieces of paper-backed fusible web on the fleece surface and fuse from the wrong side of the background fabric. Sew around the edges to secure the applique.

Sulky Puffy Foam™ can also be used to add dimension under appliques. It works best with satin stitching. Experiment with this product to discover its possibilities.

1. Cut a piece of Puffy Foam (color to match thread) slightly larger than the applique design. Place the foam on top of the background fabric so the foam is between the fabric and the applique (Fig. 32). To hold it in place, use a fusible spray on both sides of the foam.

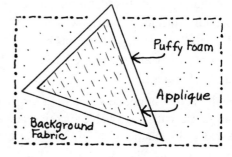

Fig. 32

2. Add stabilizer to the underside of the background fabric before stitching. The foam will be perforated by the stitching so it can be easily torn away from the outside edge of the applique. It remains in the center of the applique. The applique will be machine washable at a low temperature, but can not be dry cleaned.

In the manner of trapunto, an applique can also be stuffed from the back after it has been sewn into place. However, it must not be permanently fused to the background fabric. Consider using a fusible spray to attach the applique for this method or use Liqui-Fuse on the outer edges of the back of the applique shape.

1. After sewing around the applique, carefully cut a small opening through the back of the background fabric only (Fig. 33).

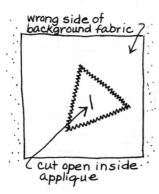

Fig. 33

2. Stuff small amounts of polyester stuffing through the opening and distribute it around the space in the applique. Hand sew the opening closed upon completion (Fig. 34).

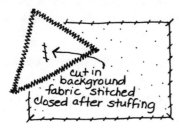

Fig. 34

Frazzled Applique

Here's where strict traditionalists in machine applique may gasp! With this technique, all edges of appliques are left untreated so they will fray. This casual look adds extra interest to the designs because the edges are also not firmly affixed to the background and the fraying adds character.

1. Trace the actual applique shape on a larger piece of woven fabric with a washable marking pen or chalk marker. Cut the shape from fabric with a 1/4" fabric allowance all the way around the shape (Fig. 35). Since the end result of this technique is a frayed look, it is not necessary to cut with precision. Once the fraying begins, the edges will be irregular anyway.

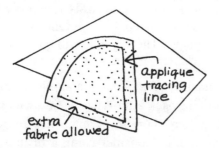

Fig. 35

2. Secure the applique to the background fabric. Use a fusible spray or pieces of fusible web only inside the area of the applique shape (Fig. 36).

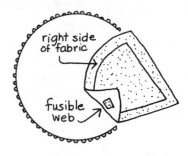

Fig. 36

3. Straight stitch around the applique on the line drawn earlier (Fig. 37). You may need a stabilizer beneath the fabrics if you use a decorative or repeating straight stitch to add prominence to the applique outline. Also consider the thread color—a contrasting thread color would make the stitching line more noticeable.

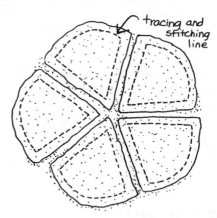

Fig. 37

4. After sewing around the applique, let the fraying happen naturally or hurry it along by washing and drying the decorated piece. To flatten the applique and edges after laundering, press the designs.

Fringed appliques are another version of frazzled applique. This time, woven fabric blocks are frayed and fringed first on all four sides. Then the fringed piece is sewn to the background. Sew a narrow zigzag stitch at the inner edge of the fringe to secure the fabric and prevent further fraying (Fig. 38).

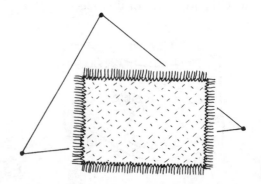

Fig. 38

See-Through Appliques

In this applique variation, the top layer of fabric is sheer. What we see through the layer depends on the fabric's sheerness.

Good fabric choices for the top layer include silk organza, netting (tulle), lace, and chiffon. Experiment by placing fabric prospects over the background fabric. Generally, these appliques will be more delicate due to the nature of the fabric. Keep in mind the potential use and abuse the finished project will be subjected to—this variation is best for protected items.

Since the edges of these fabrics are not stable, consider the edge stitching options. A wide satin stitch will cover and enclose the edges of chiffons and organza. See the Frazzled Applique technique above for ways to fray and fringe organza or sheers. Also see Framing Appliques on page 43 for other ways to cover the fabric edges. When sewing on fused sheer fabrics, check and clean the bottom of the presser foot to make sure the fusing material doesn't accumulate.

Lace fabric is an attractive choice for appliques. Use an applique pressing sheet on the ironing board while fusing paper-backed fusible web on the back of lace appliques and when fusing the lace designs to the background fabric. Another protection for both the ironing board and iron from the residue of fusing is tissue paper (the gift wrapping variety). Use it to cover the appliques before fusing them to the background. Remove it immediately after fusing and throw it away so you don't transfer the fusing residue to another project or a gift.

For another effect, cut out the background fabric behind lace and other sheer appliques. This time, completely fusing the applique will not work.

1. Trace and cut the outline of the applique shape on paper-backed fusible web. Draw a second line 1/4"

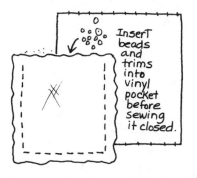

paper-backed fusible web

cut away from center of design

cut on this line

paper-backed fusible web outline fused to wrong side of applique fabric

Fig. 39

inside the tracing line and cut away the center of the shape (Fig. 39).

2. Fuse the outline to the wrong side of the applique fabric, cut out the applique, and remove the paper backing so the shape can be fused to a background.

3. Sew around the outside edges. From the back of the project, cut away inside the stitching lines (Fig. 40). If the effect is too sheer or the fabrics need support, sew or fuse a second layer of lace or netting or a piece of fabric of another color to the wrong side of the background fabric.

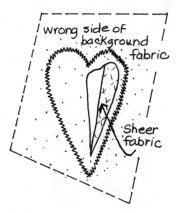

wrong side of background fabric

Sheer fabric

Fig. 40

Think of sheer fabrics as a "window" to reveal another applique shape behind. The fabric beneath the sheer should be a bright color so it will show through the translucent layer of sheer fabric over it.

Clear vinyl offers another possibility for see-through appliques. This fun idea for kids is simply squares of vinyl with small beads or flat charms free to move inside (Fig. 41).

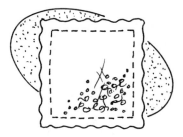

Fig. 41

Straight stitch the square on, inserting the trinkets before completing the stitching (Fig. 42).

Insert beads and trims into vinyl pocket before sewing it closed.

Fig. 42

No-Sew Appliques

Paper-backed fusible webs have made it quick and easy to attach appliques without sewing.

There are two kinds of paper-backed fusible webs, one for sewing (a lighter weight) and the other for fusing without sewing (a heavier weight that can cause sewing machine problems if you try to sew through it).

No-sew appliques can be added to surfaces that would be impossible to sew (canvas tennis shoes, purses, paper bags, etc). It is also a sensible method for applique on signs and other projects that will not have heavy wear and tear or need the extra reinforcement of sewing around the edges (Fig. 43).

Fig. 43

Follow the manufacturer's directions for either the light or heavy weight version of paper-backed fusible web you're working with. Fuse the applique shapes to background fabric or paper or wood (or whatever).

To add stitching detail, draw stitches with a fine line permanent marking pen (Fig. 44).

stitch detail drawn around design

Fig. 44

Applique has a rich history as a form of art. Many early civilizations developed motifs and techniques that are interesting even today. You may enjoy studying the historical background of applique. For a modern adaptation of the reverse applique mola technique developed by the San Blas Indians of Central America, see Jane Hill's book, *The Electric Mola*, listed in the Bibliography.

Chapter 8:

Appliques from Found Art

This category includes non-traditional appliques—things that would not usually be considered applique possibilities. They are creative surprises, pieces of "art" you find, everyday items with extraordinary potential. This chapter and list is only a beginning and an exercise in mind-expansion regarding applique.

Do you have any of these "art" pieces in your home or sewing room?

Doilies and linens. These can be old or new handkerchiefs, dresser scarves, table napkins, or parts of any of these. Your treasure stash may contain pieces of an ancestor's handiwork or new miniature doilies you couldn't resist at the craft store. Mix these pieces with traditional applique fabrics for exciting variation in dimension and presentation (Fig. 1). I believe that your deceased grandmother, a needle woman, would encourage you to use her old needlework in new ways.

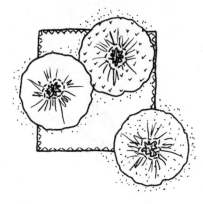

Fig. 1

Refer to See-Through Appliques on page 33 for suggestions on securing doilies to a background fabric.

Yo-yos (Fig. 2). In the past, whole quilts were made of these gathered circles of fabric. Now we can use just a few at a time to fill a basket of flowers (Fig. 3).

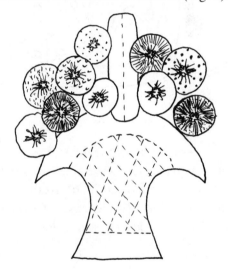

Fig. 3

Yo-yos can be purchased already completed (see resource list) or you can make your own from a 3" diameter

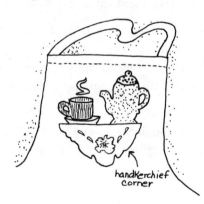

Fig. 2

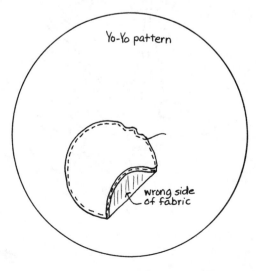

Fig. 4

circle. Turn under the edge 1/4", press, and gather by hand sewing (Fig. 4). Add a button to the center or leave as is for an attractive applique.

Gloves. Yes, I know these are not often considered as appliques, but give them a chance! You can use either summer weight gloves (crocheted or cotton) or winter one-size-fits-all stretch gloves.

Crocheted or cotton dress gloves make an attractive decoration on a pillow cover, using white or ecru fabrics for tone-on-tone trim. Add ribbons, buttons, or lace for extra accents (Fig. 5).

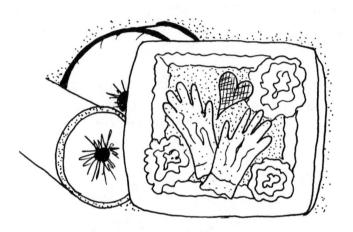

Fig. 5

Winter gloves are usually too thick to sew on as they are, so I cut away one layer. Leave a narrow seam allowance on the back of the glove (Fig. 6). At the wrist area, there are often two layers of a thicker knit. Cut most of the inside layer away, again leaving seam allowances.

You may need to clip and trim further at the corners of the wrist area to reduce the bulk (Fig. 7). Fuse the gloves to the background and sew with clear or matching thread and the blanket stitch for a hidden seam attachment.

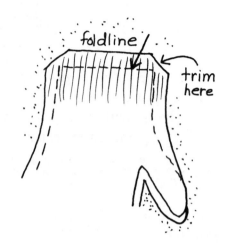

Fig. 7

Foundation piecing and quilt squares. These examples of found art may be languishing in your unfinished project box. Incidentally, this is a good box to check for other applique possibilities too. After all, if the projects have been stashed for this long, it may be a good idea to revive them for a new life.

Foundation piecing is a popular way to build pieced works for quilts, wall hangings, and Christmas ornaments. Frame one pieced square turned "on point" to the diamond position and applique it to the front of a t-shirt (Fig. 8).

Also see Celebration Squares on page 137 for another way to frame and use quilt squares as appliques.

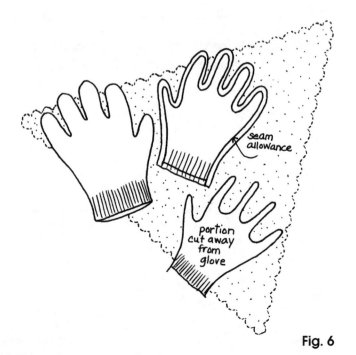

Fig. 6

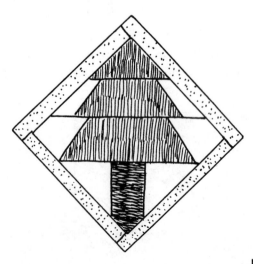

Fig. 8

Photo transfers on fabric. Make fabric copies of favorite photos, cards, or other mementos and turn them into appliques. Image transfer paper and a high thread count cotton fabric combine to produce interesting photo effects that launder well with care. Refer to the directions accompanying the design paper.

Check Applique Framing on page 43 for ideas to frame your fabric photos.

Print fabrics. This is applique work done for you. Many clever printed fabrics offer motifs and unique designs. All you have to do is cut them from the fabric, fuse them on a background, and sew around the edges (Fig. 9).

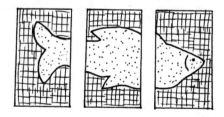

Fig. 9

Instead of sewing them on as one piece, consider cutting a printed design in three pieces and separating them (Fig. 10). This is a surprising way to display a design and adds an artistic quality to the applique. See the color photo section for an example.

Fig. 10

Silk flowers. Browse through the silk flower display at a craft store and select flowers and leaves to use as appliques. The best flowers for this project are those made of layers of silk polyester. Examples include chrysanthemums (a medium size one I took apart had eight flat layers), daisies, and dogwood. Each layer of any of these flowers can represent a flower all by itself.

1. Take the flower apart by cutting the stem to slide the petal layers off (Fig. 11). This is not a job for your sewing scissors since most stems have wire in them. Reach instead for wire cutters, pliers, or util-

ity shears. Also remove leaves to add to the design. Many leaves have plastic veins on the back which can easily be pulled off and discarded. Some flower layers need to be pressed first to flatten them. Press with an iron on the wool setting.

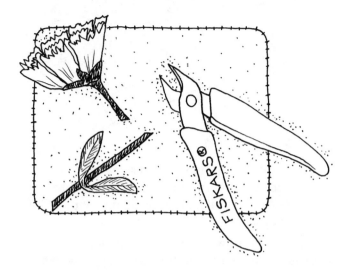

Fig. 11

2. Work on an applique pressing sheet and cut pieces of paper-backed fusible web (heavy weight only if you do *not* plan to sew on the flowers) slightly larger than the flowers or leaves. Place the flower right side down on the pressing sheet, the paper-backed fusible web with the fusible side over the flower, and fuse (Fig. 12).

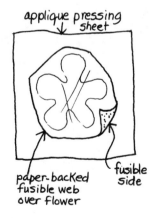

Fig. 12

3. Lift the corner of the paper backing to remove it and peel the flower or leaf off the sheet. Pick off the small pieces of fusible clinging to the flower edges.

4. Wipe the applique sheet to remove the residue from the sheet. Be sure to do this immediately so you won't transfer the residue to something else.

5. Arrange the flowers and leaves on the background

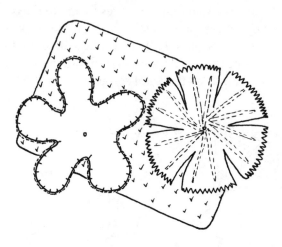

Fig. 13

fabric, place the applique pressing sheet over the top and, with the iron on the pressing sheet, fuse the designs in place. Once again, wipe off the pressing sheet.

6. To sew the flower and leaves, stabilize the background and stitch around the edges with clear thread and the blanket or blind hem stitch, or straight stitch backwards and forwards around the flower, sewing on each petal (Fig. 13).

7. There is a very small hole in the center of each flower and also in some leaf pairs. Once the designs are fused and stitched onto fabric, the holes diminish in size and are not very noticeable. To cover them, cut a piece from another flower to fuse under the hole, or cover the center with a button or buttons.

8. To launder the finished work, it is best to wash by hand and also to turn the item inside out to protect the flowers.

Scarves. Designs printed on scarves provide another unexpected source for appliques. Check your collection of old scarves or shop for a scarf to cut apart for appliques. My preference is scarves with designs easy to cut out without many jagged edges.

For a very sheer chiffon scarf, test different brands of paper-backed fusible webs to see if the finished effect is different. In my testing, Pellon's Wonder-Under produced a less shiny surface on the appliques after they were fused to the background.

Fuse the paper-backed fusible web, slightly larger than the design, over the design area on the wrong side of the scarf. To avoid distorting thin scarf fabrics, pull a corner of the paper backing from a small portion of the design area before cutting out the shape. This will give you a paper edge to grab and continue removing the paper backing after cutting out the design.

Select a stitch to cover and secure the edge of the applique. Try a wider satin stitch or satin stitch variation for the best protection of fragile, easily frayed scarf edges.

> **Where to look for applique design ideas:**
> * **Wallpaper pattern books**
> * **Stained glass design books**
> * **Paper towels with designs printed on them**
> * **Vinyl flooring patterns**
> * **Coloring books (Only the simplest ones—most have too much detail in the designs. Also, be careful about reproducing licensed designs. It's not legal.)**

Chapter 9:

Machine Embroideries & Stitches as Appliques

One of the most impressive features of new top-of-the-line sewing machines and specialty embroidery machines is their ability to automatically stitch stylish embroidered designs. Many sewing artists have experimented with the designs and look for new ways to use them. I look at the designs as a source of distinctive appliques. Actually, many machines have design cards that feature appliques.

Fringed patch. Paying attention to what's on the clothing store racks pays off in the inspiration department. Here's an idea from ready-to-wear.

1. Stitch an embroidery on a piece of woven fabric large enough to hoop. Remove the stabilizer from the back and cut the fabric into a square or rectangle 2" larger on all sides than the design (Fig. 1).

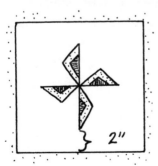

Fig. 1

2. Fringe the edges approximately 1/2". Sew the fringed fabric patch to the background as an applique, stitching a narrow zigzag stitch at the inside edge of the fringe (Fig. 2).

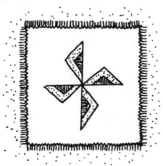

Fig. 2

If fringe is not your style, follow the same procedure but turn under the edges of the fabric and sew the design to a background with decorative stitching and contrasting color thread, or use clear thread and a blind hem or blanket stitch for a nearly invisible seam (Fig. 3).

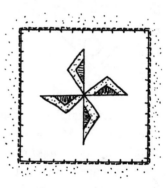

Fig. 3

Project label. Turn an embroidery into a garment or project label. After sewing the design, add your name to the fabric by stitching it on the sewing machine or writing it on with a permanent marking pen (Fig. 4). Signing your fabric work of art is an important detail. Why not do it with decorative flair?

Fig. 4

Embroideries can also be highlighted with the framing ideas explained in Applique Framing on page 43. In addition, the Celebration Squares button-on applique system on page 137 presents another way to use embroidered squares (Fig. 5).

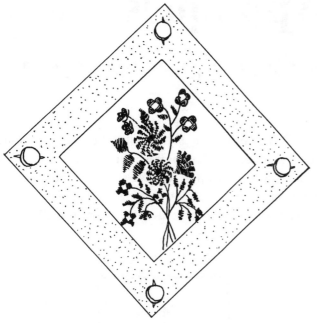

Fig. 5

Sewing machine stitch samplers can also be turned into interesting appliques (Fig. 6). Sew rows of decorative stitches on stabilized fabric, making each row a different stitch. Then cut a shape from the stitched fabric. It now becomes an applique textured by the stitches.

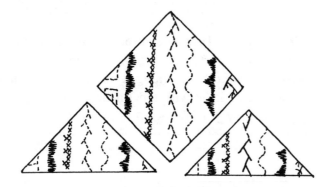

Fig. 6

What other ideas do you have for embroideries and stitches?

Things to decorate with applique—and you don't have to sew them first!

* Sweatshirts
* Baby bibs
* T-shirts
* Curtains
* Sweaters
* Toilet seat covers (mine has appliques!)
* Jackets
* Place mats and napkins
* Tote bags
* Hats
* Vests
* Christmas tree skirts
* Cuffs and collars
* Blankets
* Dresses
* Mail box cloth covers
* Pillows
* Backpacks
* Aprons
* Chair covers
* Book covers
* Anything that stands still!

Chapter 10:

Applique Enhancements

Combine applique with other elements to add dimensional details and style to your creations.

Buttons are an easy favorite choice. They can be used to represent details such as the tires on a truck design for a child, centers of flowers, or as trim sprinkled around a design (Fig. 1). Sew them on by hand or machine or use shank buttons which can be attached with what I call the golden metallic method of button attachment—safety pins! Securing buttons in this way allows changing your mind about button choice and placement as well as removal for laundering.

Fig. 1

Another way to attach buttons temporarily is to pin or sew narrow ribbons or yarn to the fabric, pull the ribbons through the button openings, and tie the buttons to the applique (Fig. 2).

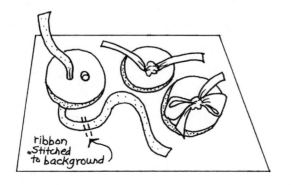

Fig. 2

Metal charms also make great trims for applique. They can often be attached as buttons are, or tied on with ribbon (Fig. 3).

Fig. 3

Metal and plastic snaps offer another choice for dimensional accents. Use the snap halves for eyes on animals or human faces, for flower centers, or other details (Fig. 4).

Fig. 4

Yarn or decorative thread couching is one of my favorite ways to add texture and interest to appliques. This is the process of stitching yarns or heavy threads over the top of an applique. After completing the applique stitching, leave the stabilizer on the back of the fabric. Plan the placement of the yarn and mark the lines with a chalk marker or washable marking pen. Use clear nylon thread for stitching that is hidden in

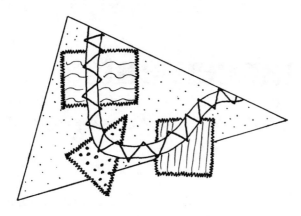

Fig. 5

the yarn, and select a zigzag stitch width that will cross over the yarn without piercing it (Fig. 5).

Begin by sewing back and forth over the end of the yarn and then proceed to sew the yarn on the lines drawn for a pattern. Secure the end of the yarn by stitching back and forth over the end (Fig. 6). Remove the stabilizer after couching is completed.

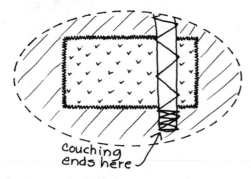

Couching ends here

Fig. 6

Silk embroidery by machine or hand is a popular technique for embellishments and enhanced appliques. It's a great combination with extra dimension created by the embroidery.

Hand stitching adds character to appliques. The stitching can "echo" around a shape or be added inside the shape for a quilted look. It is most effective on appliques attached with a hidden machine stitch along the edges. Less-than-perfect hand stitches can give a distinct country/rustic flavor to an applique (Fig. 7).

Fig. 7

Decorative trims, braids, cross-locked beads, and strings of sequins are easy additions to appliques. They can frame appliques or add detail in flowers and leaves (Fig. 8). Another product to use for flower stem and leaf details is narrow 1/4" fusible bias tape.

Sequins

Fig. 8

What creative choices can you add to this list?

Chapter 11:

Framing Appliques

Compare the difference: Applique any simple design to a background fabric and then plan a frame for the same design before sewing it in place. Which applique is more appealing and interesting? Most framed designs will be more striking and prominent than unframed ones (Fig. 1).

Fig. 1

Use the frame shapes in this section or develop your own from these ideas.

Squares as frames. Placing a square of fabric behind a design is a simple frame solution (Fig. 2).

Fig. 2

Add a second square beneath it "on point" (Fig. 3).

Fig. 3

Now try the same squares turned off their straight alignment (Fig. 4).

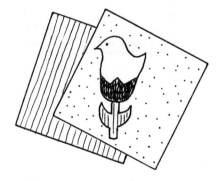

Fig. 4

Fabric strips. A standard frame is made of four strips of material. Let's consider some other arrangements with strips. Make them longer than the frame size and overlap them (Fig. 5).

Fig. 5

Use only two strips to frame the design on two sides (Fig. 8).

Fig. 6

Make them of different widths and sizes for a not-so-balanced effect (Fig. 6).

Use decorative trim as strips and extend each end (Fig. 7).

Fig. 8

Use strips from old blue jeans, bias tape, or non-fray fabrics cut with a wavy edge rotary cutter or pinking shears (Fig. 9).

Fig. 9

Fig. 7

As you can see, frames do not have to be traditional or ordinary, but they can make a wonderful difference in the presentation of a simple applique design. Start your own applique framing career today.

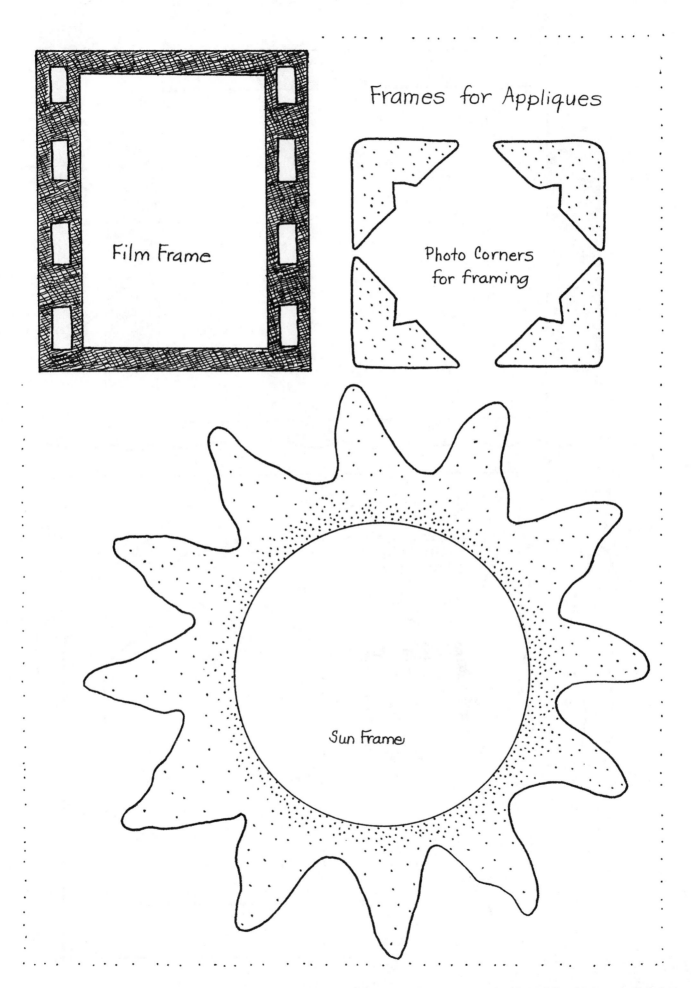

Film Frame

Frames for Appliques

Photo Corners
for framing

Sun Frame

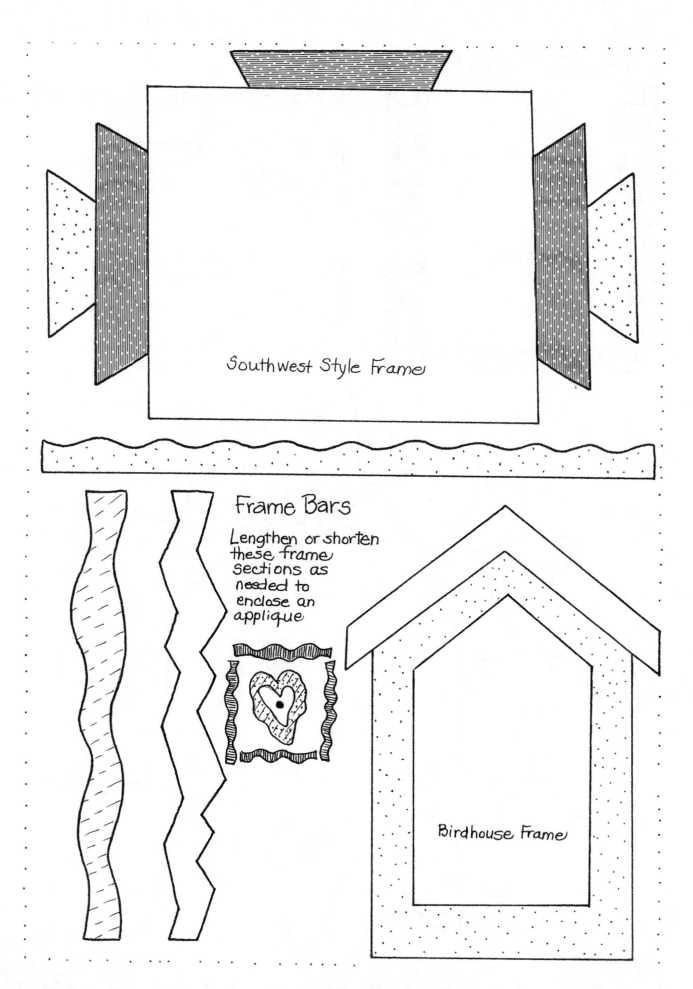

Southwest Style Frame

Frame Bars

Lengthen or shorten these frame sections as needed to enclose an applique

Birdhouse Frame

Chapter 12:

Applique Design Placement on Garments for Women

Location, location, location! It's as important in garment embellishment as it is in real estate.

Anyone who has attended my seminars knows that my recurring theme is the planning of design placement on clothing for women. This step is crucial to successful and classy embellished garments.

It is essential to plan the design location after marking the bustline and ends of the shoulders when the garment is on a body (Fig. 1). Make these marks with pins or a washable marking pen, then plan the design layout and pin the shapes in place.

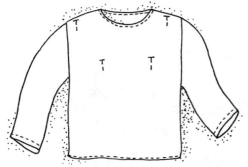

Fig. 1

Try the garment on again to test the layout. Critical areas to check are the sides of garments where folds in the fabric can distort applique designs (Fig. 2). This detail is impossible to check when the garment is flat on a table.

Fig. 2

Designs located in the yoke of the shirt, above the bustline and between the shoulders, are usually in a safe area (Fig. 3). This is also a flattering placement because the design frames the head so the viewer's eye sees the design and then is drawn up to the face.

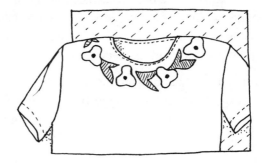

Fig. 3

Another successful design placement is the diagonal line across a garment. It begins at one shoulder and moves diagonally across the garment and body. This is a flattering line for both large and small bodies (Fig. 4). Again, avoid placing prominent designs directly on the bustline.

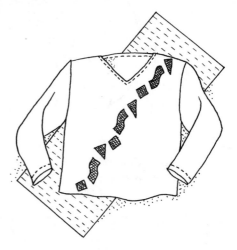

Fig. 4

The time spent in planning and testing design layouts is never wasted and is certain to result in a stylish applique design for any woman's garment.

Chapter 13:

Care & Laundering of Appliques

Taking good care of all projects and garments decorated with appliques pays off in a long and attractive life for your embellishments.

If the piece can be laundered, it is best to turn it inside out. Hand washing in cool to warm water is also advised. This agitates the design surface much less than the automatic washer. If the piece is machine washed, place it inside out in a lingerie bag or closed pillowcase to protect the garment and the decorations.

Should you dry an appliqued piece in the dryer? Air drying is best. However, my suggestion for using the dryer is for only a few minutes to tumble out the major wrinkles in the fabric. The dryer temperature should be cool or warm, but not hot. Note that the manufacturers of fusible webs, interfacings, and other products used in applique recommend laundering and drying temperatures in the cool to warm range. After a few minutes in the dryer, remove the piece to air dry.

Before the garment or accessory is used again, expect to iron it. Most appliques look best with touch-up pressing on both the right and wrong sides. Use a press cloth over appliques of iron-sensitive fabrics.

Chapter 14:

Designing Your Own Appliques

Don't let this chapter title scare you away. Anyone can be a designer, even you!

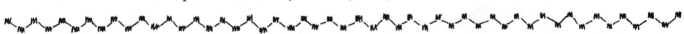

Start with a few simple geometric shapes like the squares and triangles at the end of this chapter. Cut several from paper in the colors you plan to use or from scrap fabrics.

Select the item you plan to decorate. Read my advice on marking women's garments (page 47) before planning applique designs. Begin by laying out just a few of the shapes and then add more to build a design.

If an orderly balanced design appeals to you, arrange the squares and triangles in straight rows, a rectangle, or a circle (Fig. 1). Also see the nine-patch layout in the color photo section on page 80.

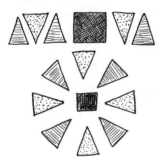

Fig. 1

You may discover that a more artistic design and arrangement develops with an unbalanced arrangement and the introduction of another shape such as a bar (Fig. 2).

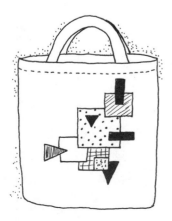

Fig. 2

Change the sizes of the shapes you're working with if they appear too small or large on the surface you're decorating. On a vest, consider trimming only one side of the front or decorate both sides differently (Fig. 3).

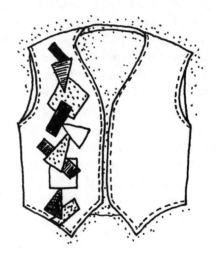

Fig. 3

It will take practice and experimentation to get comfortable as an applique layout designer. Arrange and then study your design layouts. This is easiest to do if the piece can be hung on a wall or bulletin board and you can get a distance away to see the total effect. Ask for opinions from others, even non-sewing people in your family or workplace. Study well-designed ready-to-wear for inspiration. Collect pictures from magazines and catalogs. Work at being a designer of appliques and then don't be surprised when you hear compliments on your artistic sewing creations.

Scrap Appliques: Here's a new way to build artistic appliques from scraps of fabric and yarn. For this project, you'll need netting (tulle), water soluble stabilizer, and clear nylon thread.

1. Place a piece of water soluble stabilizer on a work surface with a piece of tulle the same size on top. Cut out pieces of fabric all in one color family, or a random collection of colors. Arrange the pieces on the tulle, overlapping them. You can leave some gaps in the arrangement so the background fabric will show through (Fig. 4).

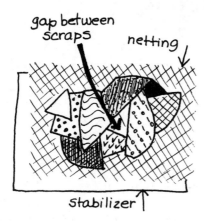

gap between scraps

netting

stabilizer

Fig. 4

2. Over the top of the fabrics, lay pieces of yarn to meander across, around, or under the scraps. When the layout pleases you, place a piece of water soluble stabilizer over the top. Pin all the layers together. (For additional holding power, use fusible spray on each layer of water soluble stabilizer to better hold all the layers and pieces together.)

3. With clear nylon thread on top and bobbin thread to match or blend with the fabric colors, sew through all layers of the piece, sewing straight forward and backward until you have secured all the pieces and yarns. It will be easy to see through the stabilizer (Fig. 5).

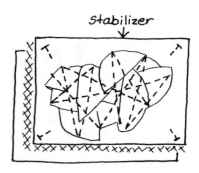

stabilizer

Fig. 5

4. Dissolve the stabilizer by holding the stitched piece under running water and then soaking it in water to remove all traces of the stabilizer. If the piece dries and still feels stiff, soak it longer. Hang the piece to dry.

5. Set the iron temperature at the wool (medium) setting to iron the piece and prevent the tulle from shrinking. (Ask me how I know this!)

6. Cut an applique shape from this new piece of fabric or use the whole piece as an applique. Trim away the extra tulle and fuse the shape to the background fabric. Fusible spray works well, or fuse strips of paper-backed fusible web on the edges or the entire back surface.

7. Position the design shape on the background and then sew it in place with clear nylon thread and a zigzag stitch or the scrub cover stitch as described on page 26. Wait till you hear them rave about this design creation!

Design Collection

Abstract Designs

See this design in the color photo section.

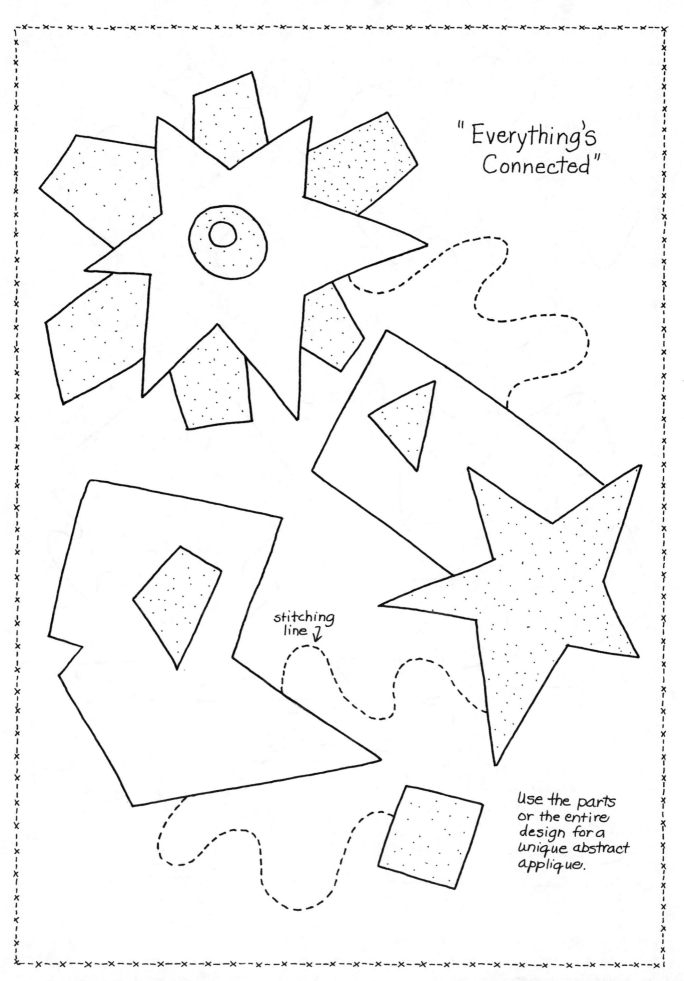

"Everything's Connected"

stitching line

Use the parts or the entire design for a unique abstract applique.

Pieces
of the
Puzzle

Lines, Spots, and Shapes

Shapes Worth Repeating

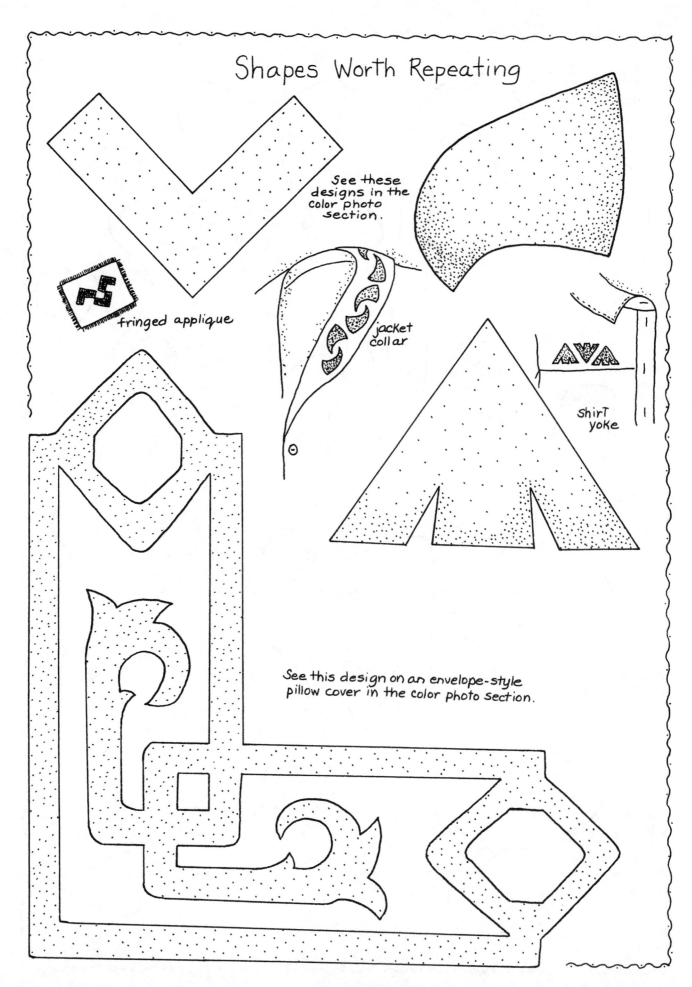

See these designs in the color photo section.

fringed applique

jacket collar

shirt yoke

See this design on an envelope-style pillow cover in the color photo section.

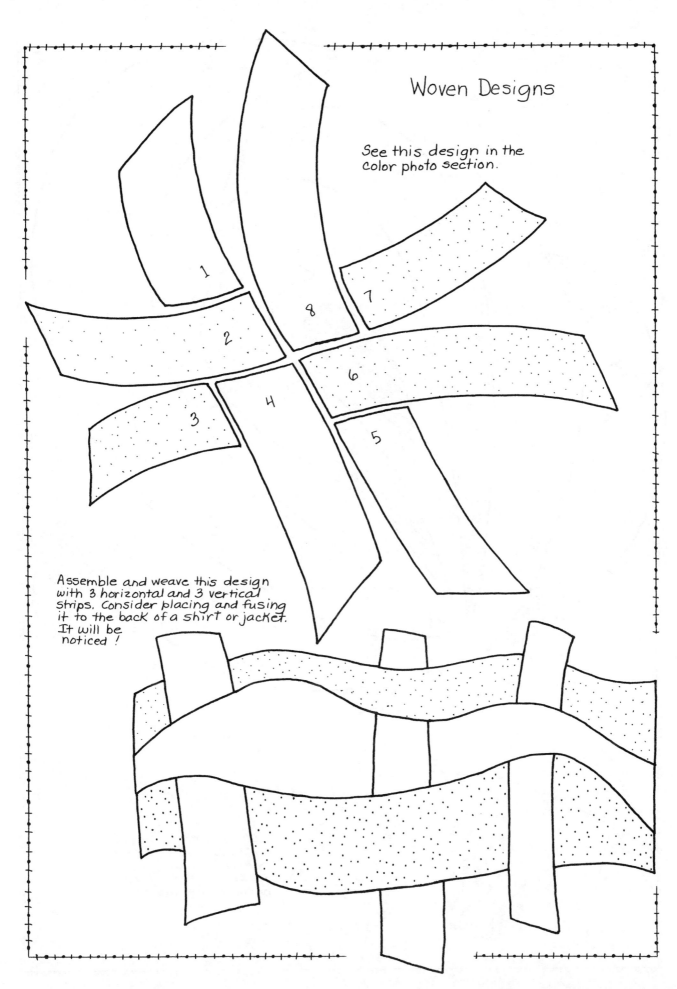

Woven Designs

See this design in the color photo section.

Assemble and weave this design with 3 horizontal and 3 vertical strips. Consider placing and fusing it to the back of a shirt or jacket. It will be noticed!

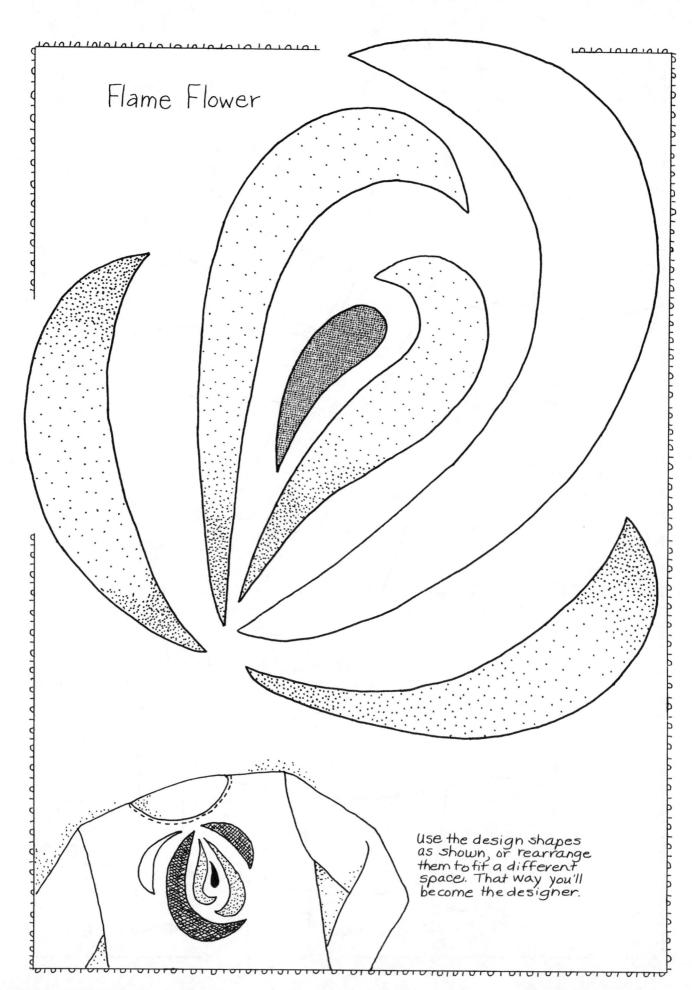

Flame Flower

Use the design shapes as shown, or rearrange them to fit a different space. That way you'll become the designer.

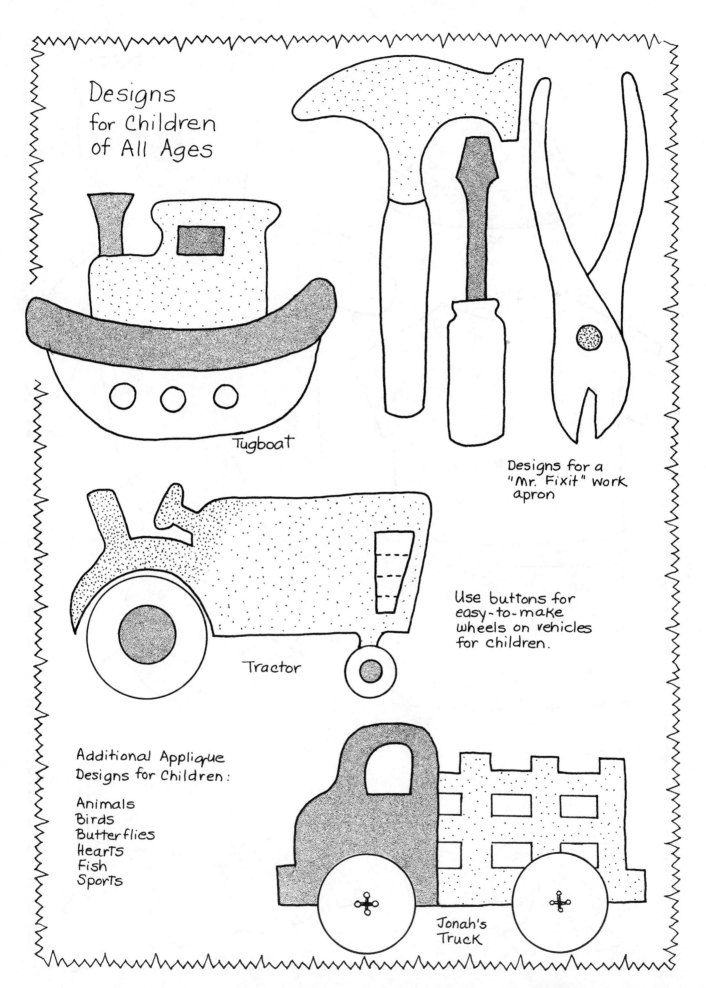

Designs
for Children
of All Ages

Tugboat

Designs for a
"Mr. Fixit" work
apron

Use buttons for
easy-to-make
wheels on vehicles
for children.

Tractor

Additional Applique
Designs for Children:

Animals
Birds
Butterflies
Hearts
Fish
Sports

Jonah's
Truck

Dress the Teddy Bear

Hat

T-Shirt or Vest

Shorts

Bowtie

Bow

Dress

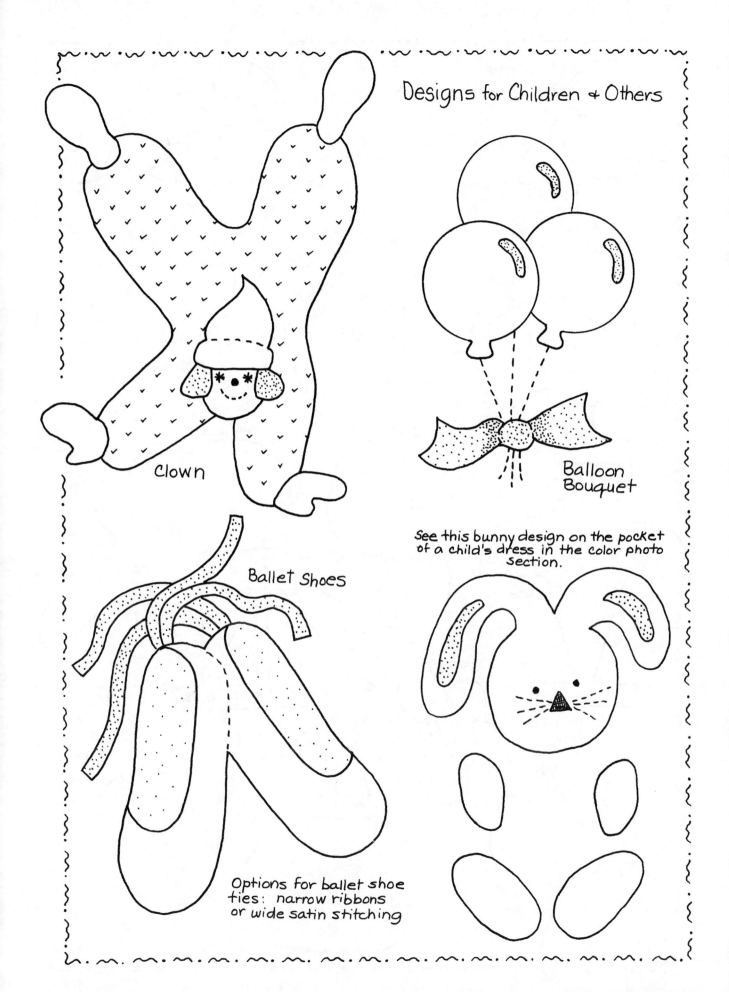

Designs for Children & Others

Clown

Balloon Bouquet

See this bunny design on the pocket of a child's dress in the color photo section.

Ballet Shoes

Options for ballet shoe ties: narrow ribbons or wide satin stitching

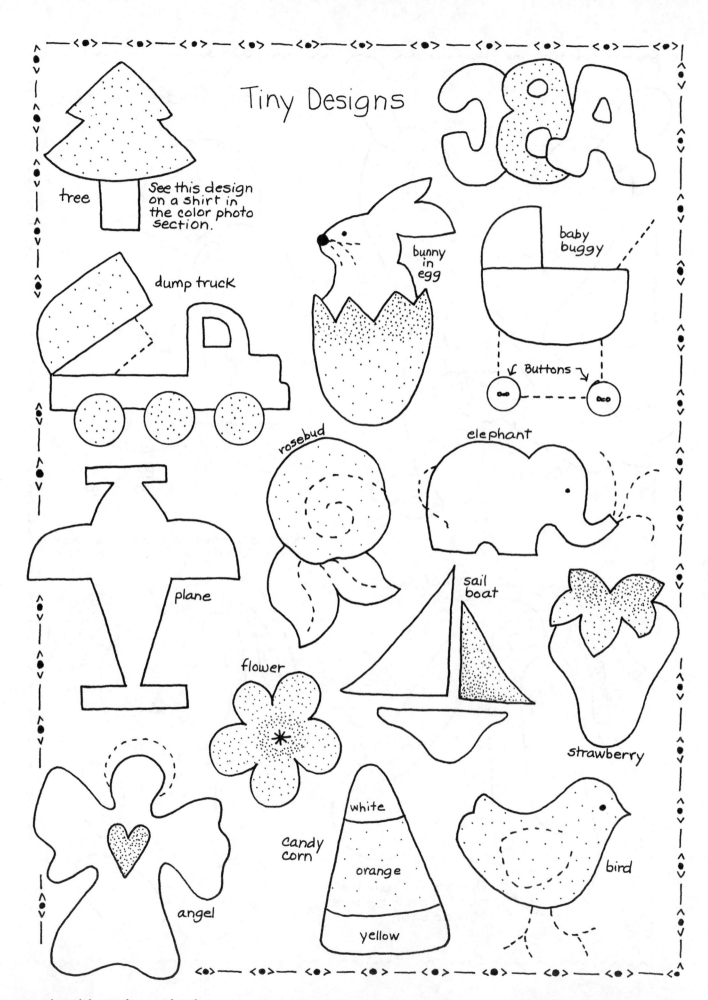

Tiny Designs

tree

See this design on a shirt in the color photo section.

dump truck

bunny in egg

baby buggy

Buttons

rosebud

elephant

plane

sail boat

flower

strawberry

angel

candy corn

white

orange

yellow

bird

Pie and Coffee

Pie and coffee – a real minnesota afternoon treat!

See this design on an apron in the color photo section. I used a handkerchief corner for the tablecloth part of this design.

See this design on an apron in the color photo section. I used fleece fabric for the whipped cream on the slice of pie.

white

tan

the color of your favorite pie

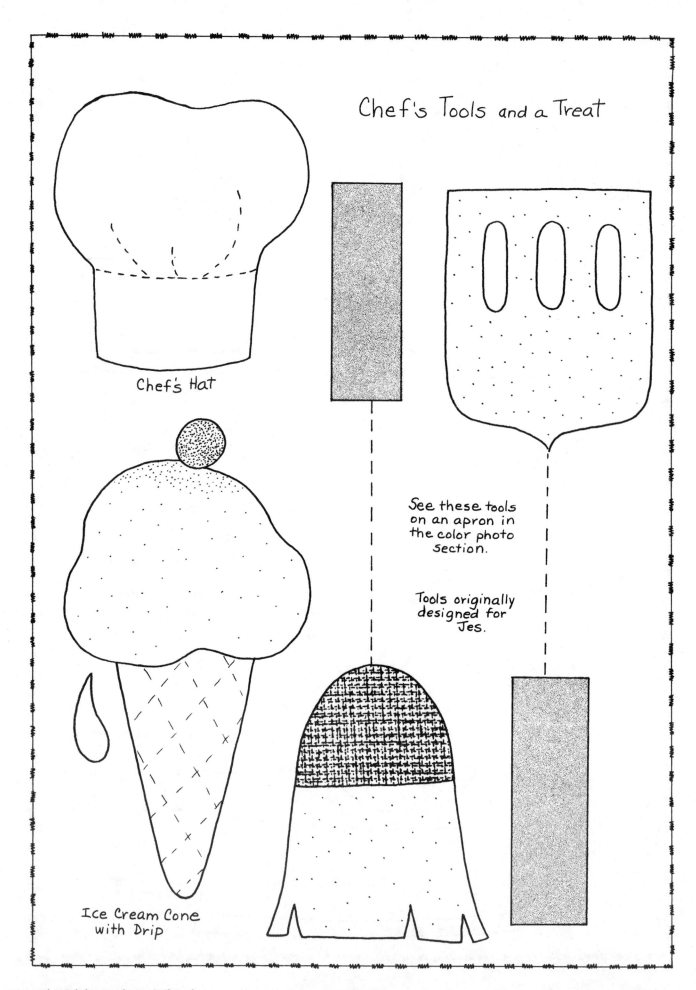

Chef's Tools and a Treat

Chef's Hat

See these tools
on an apron in
the color photo
section.

Tools originally
designed for
Jes.

Ice Cream Cone
with Drip

❧ Applique Design Gallery ❧

A colorful scarf provided the applique shapes for an orange t-shirt. The squares and rectangles cut from the scarf were fused on and sewn with a wide satin stitch around the edges. Decorative machine stitching was added inside each applique and the square at the center front features bar tack applique. I chose a lightweight cut-away stabilizer for the back of the t-shirt so I would not rip away the stabilizer and ruin the stitches.

Several shades of peach Ultrasuede provided tone-on-tone appliques for this peach shirt. I used cotton embroidery thread and the blanket stitch to sew each leaf. After all the appliques and stitching added such a classy touch to the shirt, I removed the ordinary buttons that came on the shirt and replaced them with new buttons.

Here's a great way to show off the embroideries from your sewing machine—turn them into Celebration Squares! I surrounded each embroidery with an Ultrasuede frame cut with a wavy edge rotary cutter and buttoned it on a garment or accessory. The machine companies represented by the embroideries are, clockwise from upper left: Viking, Pfaff, New Home, Singer, Babylock, and Bernina.

Here are two ways to prepare Celebration Squares to wear and carry. The apron on the left features a no-sew example using felt. I fused tricot interfacing to stabilize and strengthen the back of the felt base for the design. Buttonholes were an easy single cut in the felt—no sewing required. The shamrock square is an example of lined applique with netting used to line the cotton fabric of the shamrock. The fun part of these squares is that you can unbutton them from one item and button them on another.

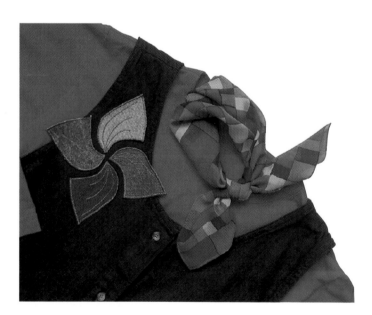

Pieces of old blue jeans provided the fabric for the "liberated" appliques trimming this jumper. Both the right and wrong sides of the denim were used. I chose twist rayon thread by Coats for both the edge stitching and the straight stitching which anchors the shapes to the jumper.

A perfect gift for the golfer: a plain terrycloth towel trimmed with a golf applique. I chose a dark color for the towel so the golfer could use it as a bag towel without fear of stain and ruin!

The same fabrics used to trim the color-blocked jacket below were snipped off and used to compose a scrap applique for this t-shirt. Now I can wear the t-shirt and jacket together for a neatly coordinated outfit. And to think it's only scraps of fabric and a piece of yarn wound over the top!

A simple v-shaped applique trims this purchased jacket. I used a combination of denim/chambray woven fabrics for the appliques on the collar and the jacket front and back yoke too. Don't forget to trim the back of your clothing.

A plain pillow cover from Bagworks gets style and class with parts taken from silk flowers. The flower layers and leaves were fused on the pillow cover and then to hold them firmly in place, I blanket stitched around the leaves and straight stitched back and forth from the center to the edges of the flowers. The colors and shading of silk flowers provide elegance to this "found art" form of applique.

On this envelope-style pillow cover from Bagworks, an Ultrasuede corner applique adds a touch of style. The pillow cover's original button was replaced with one to coordinate with the design fabric and color.

A variety of satin stitches and satin stitch extensions cover the edges of the stars on this folding chair back cover. Small star embroidered appliques add extra trim. Embellished covers for folding chairs are an easy and clever way to make an ordinary chair much more appealing.

This see-through applique features black silk organza wings satin stitched to the background fabric. After stitching, the background fabric was carefully cut away on the back inside the wings.

Why use plain kitchen towels when decorated ones are quick to produce and much more interesting! The pink and tan towel features an appliqued basket with purchased fabric yo-yos from Wimpole Street Creations. Three pieces of fruit, each in a fabric frame, trim the tan towel. The frame edges were cut with a pinking shears and will fray with use and laundering. (In our new world of applique, it's okay if fabrics fray!)

My first foundation piecing project was gathering dust in a drawer when I rediscovered it as "found art" for applique. Positioned and sewn "on point" on the back of a vest, it presents an eye-catching embellishment.

Lycra fabrics are great non-fray choices for appliques. The lustrous shine of the fabric adds appeal to the design. Use this apron applique idea for your favorite barbecue chef.

A variety of pink fabrics were selected to match and blend with the bright jacket for tone-on-tone appliques of quilting shapes: squares, diamonds, and clamshells. After the (liberated) appliques were sewn to the jacket, I hand stitched around the path of shapes running diagonally across the jacket and onto the sleeve.

(Below) Easy-to-make octagon flowers trim a denim hat for a summer picnic. Cover the centers of the two layer flowers with miniature doilies, buttons, or pom poms to add more dimension and interest. I chose to attach my flowers and leaves with the "gold metallic system," often called safety pins. Then I can quickly remove them and pin them to a jumper or a sweatshirt or a tote bag.

A simple heart design trims this little girl's dress. The center of the design is cut from clear vinyl and inside the vinyl window is a collection of children's buttons with the shanks cut off. Straight stitch the vinyl on the dress and insert the trims before stitching the heart closed. Then apply fusible spray to the wrong side of the outline heart, keeping in mind that this project cannot be fused and pressed as we often do in applique. Stitch the heart outline edges over the top of the vinyl pocket. This dress is sure to be a little girl pleaser.

The highlight on the pocket of a sturdy canvas tote is a Canada goose applique. This design is a great choice for a bird watcher or naturalist. Just make sure you accurately call it a Canada goose.

One simple leaf design is highlighted here with two fabric frames. The outer frame is fringed. For additional interest, the leaf is padded with Puffy Foam.

Deep pink rose appliques trim a gray t-shirt, adding a touch of style. The center detail of each flower is stitched on with metallic thread for a bit of sparkle. The same design was also used in a reduced size for the denim dress shown in this color photo section.

An overlapping diamond design was selected for this man's sweatshirt. I chose imitation suede fabrics and used an irregular edge satin stitch for the center diamond.

A collection of my mother's childhood Valentines inspired this pillow trim. I photocopied the Valentines on image transfer paper and then ironed the designs onto fabric. It's a great way to share the sweet designs and Valentine greetings while preserving the actual cards. For extra trim, I sewed on small heart buttons and added a red bow to complete the Valentine theme.

A plain dress with a pocket becomes a child's garment of style with the addition of a rabbit surrounding the pocket. Ultrasuede was chosen for its ease in laundering and drying, its soft touch for children, and its durability.

A combination of geometric shapes trims the ends of a table runner. Fusible gold bias tape covers the edges of each shape. I stitched the bias tape in place using a double needle, clear nylon thread, and a small zigzag stitch.

Choose a fabric color to match someone's favorite cat and you're sure to create a pleasing applique on a backpack or other accessory. The cat is framed with pinked edge fabric which will fray with wear and time. (Backpack from Bagworks.)

Fuse fabric appliques on bags, note cards, and signs—sewing is not required. Just remember to fuse with a dry iron—no steam.

Red and green Ultrasuede were natural color choices for applique on this Christmas card holder. The holly leaves and berries were straight stitched to the background and the frame serves to accent the holiday design.

A tiny tree design repeated on the shirt's collar, cuffs, and front placket makes a bold and interesting statement on a plain chambray shirt.

A fish design from a piece of printed fabric makes a unique applique after it is cut into thirds. Woven trim and an additional strip of fabric under the fish pieces make this applique design extraordinary.

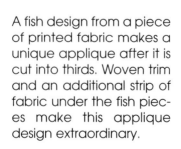

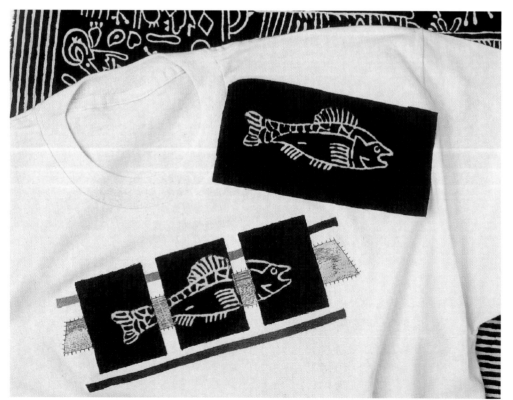

It's fun to combine old and new fabrics for applique. A vintage handkerchief provided the tablecloth corner for this apron applique and new cotton fabrics from P & B Textiles were chosen for the pot and cup.

(Left) The flower designs on the jacket lapel and front were traced and cut from velour fabric, layered over the original designs, and stitched on as overlay appliques. This technique adds another layer of interest to printed fabric.

(Right) A fringed denim square frames the Carolina Lily applique on this sweatshirt. It's a great design for a quilter or a "country" enthusiast.

An abstract applique shape surrounded by echo stitching highlights the side of a vest. I chose a textured knit fabric for the applique and after stitching it to the vest, I sewed around the design with a decorative machine stitch and Sulky rayon thread. I found that drawing a line to follow around the design was very helpful.

(Below) A combination of textured imitation suede and Ultrasuede fabrics produces the look of a real baseball glove, bat, and ball. The red stitching on the ball adds more realistic detail.

The best and only way to become a professional applique satin stitcher is to practice. Try different stitch widths and lengths on your sewing machine and then practice sewing around a design with curves, straight edges, points, and corners. The more you practice, the better your stitching will be.

For the pie baking expert, what better applique choice than a slice of pie? Cotton fabrics were chosen for the pie and thin fusible fleece became the spot of whipped cream atop the pie. This slice of blueberry pie is for my husband Barry, the pie baker at our house.

For the best design visibility, trim a place mat in the space above the plate. I used parts of the same flower applique to decorate the napkin and complete the place setting.

A zip tote bag from Bagworks becomes stylish with reverse applique diamonds. Two cotton Hoffman print fabrics were stitched to the wrong side of the bag front and then the denim was cut away from the stitching lines. To stabilize the cotton fabrics, I fused lightweight fusible interfacing to the wrong sides.

A tour through your sewing room and home can produce unusual new choices for applique beyond the traditional fabric choices. In the "Found Art" chapter, you'll find instructions for using these new choices and accents to create new forms of applique.

(Below) Hand-dyed cotton fabrics were selected for this tone-on-tone design for a maroon blouse. The edges of the woven design pieces were serged and the design was assembled and stitched to the blouse. The subtle applique adds classy appeal to the otherwise plain garment.

"Found" Art to Applique

Choose Ultrasuede for a sturdy and stylish book cover. An additional strip of Ultrasuede was sewn on for a bookmark. The applique chosen for this Bible cover is the lily of the valley design, with the flower stems stitched with a wide satin stitch and the Ultrasuede shapes straight stitched to the book cover.

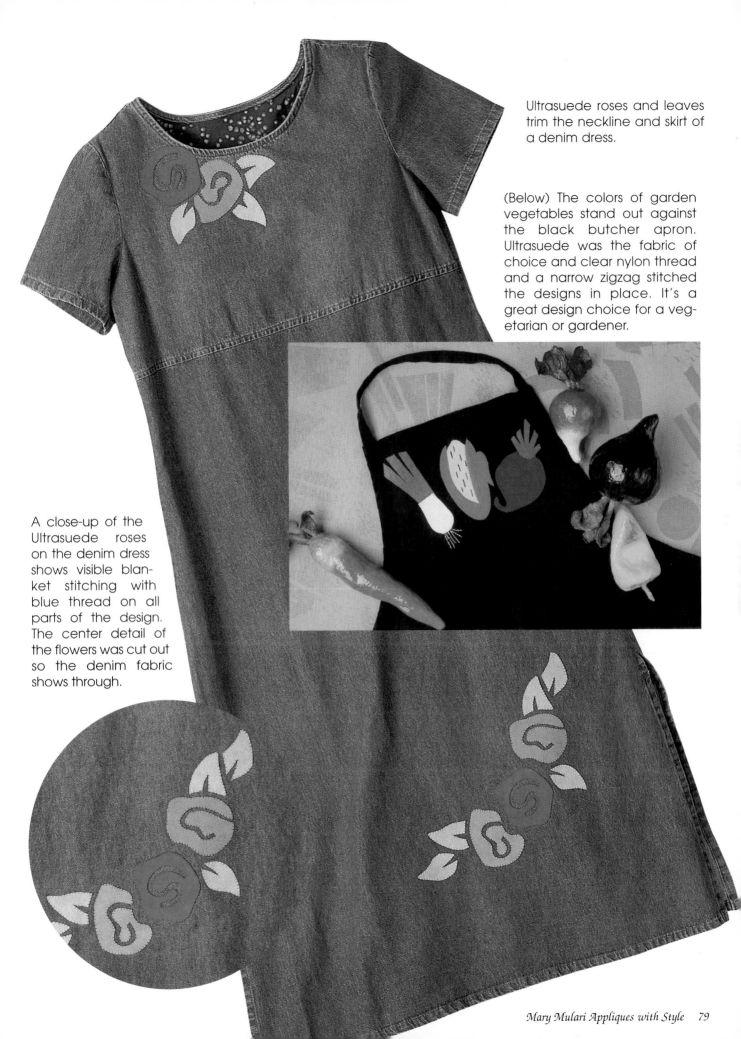

Ultrasuede roses and leaves trim the neckline and skirt of a denim dress.

(Below) The colors of garden vegetables stand out against the black butcher apron. Ultrasuede was the fabric of choice and clear nylon thread and a narrow zigzag stitched the designs in place. It's a great design choice for a vegetarian or gardener.

A close-up of the Ultrasuede roses on the denim dress shows visible blanket stitching with blue thread on all parts of the design. The center detail of the flowers was cut out so the denim fabric shows through.

Black and white fabrics and pieces of yarn compose the scrap applique on this jacket's back yoke. This creative and easy applique technique produces artistic results that are sure to be noticed.

This nine-patch design features many of the new ways to applique. The top row, from left to right, shows traditional satin stitch applique, scrub cover applique, and blanket stitch applique. Row two shows lined applique, invisible applique, and couched applique. Row three presents decorative stitch applique, reverse applique, and a satin stitch variation.

After sewing all the appliqued items you see in these pictures, I schedule a day with the photographer, Gerry Tucker. Then it seems as if I load the entire contents of my home into the car! At the end of the day, here I am with most of what I brought for photos and props, along with the photographer's equipment. It's an exhausting day, but an important one for this book.

Angels

Use these appliques for a December holiday sweatshirt or a garment or accessory for any time of year.

Heavenly
Designs

Heavenly Designs

1 2

3

8

9

7

6

5

4

Hint: Number the sun rays with the same numbers when you trace the design on paper-backed fusible web.

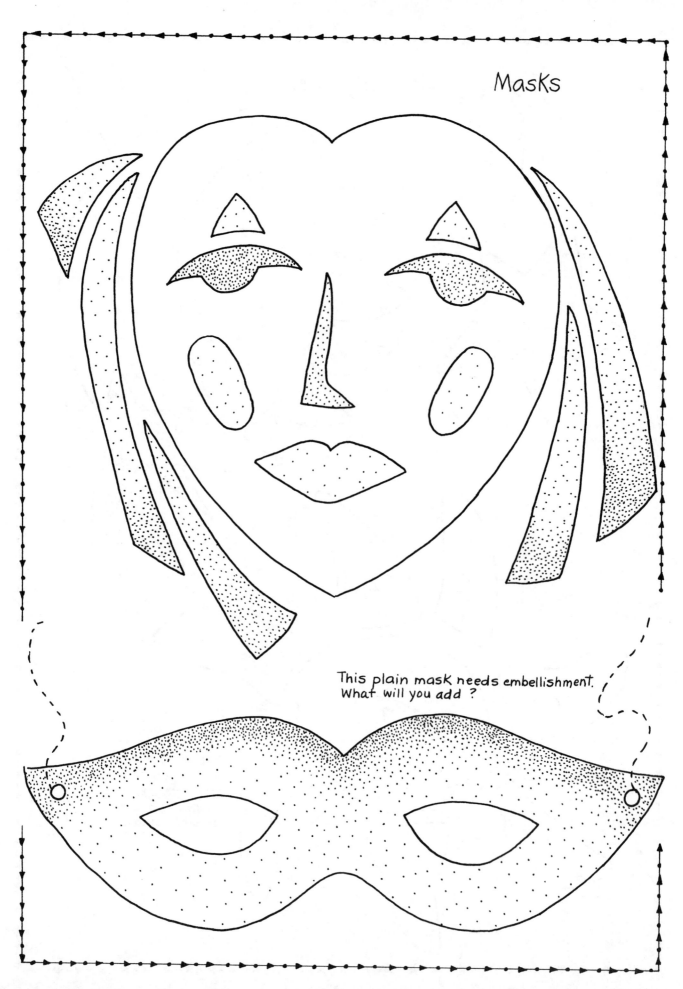

Masks

This plain mask needs embellishment.
What will you add?

Primitives

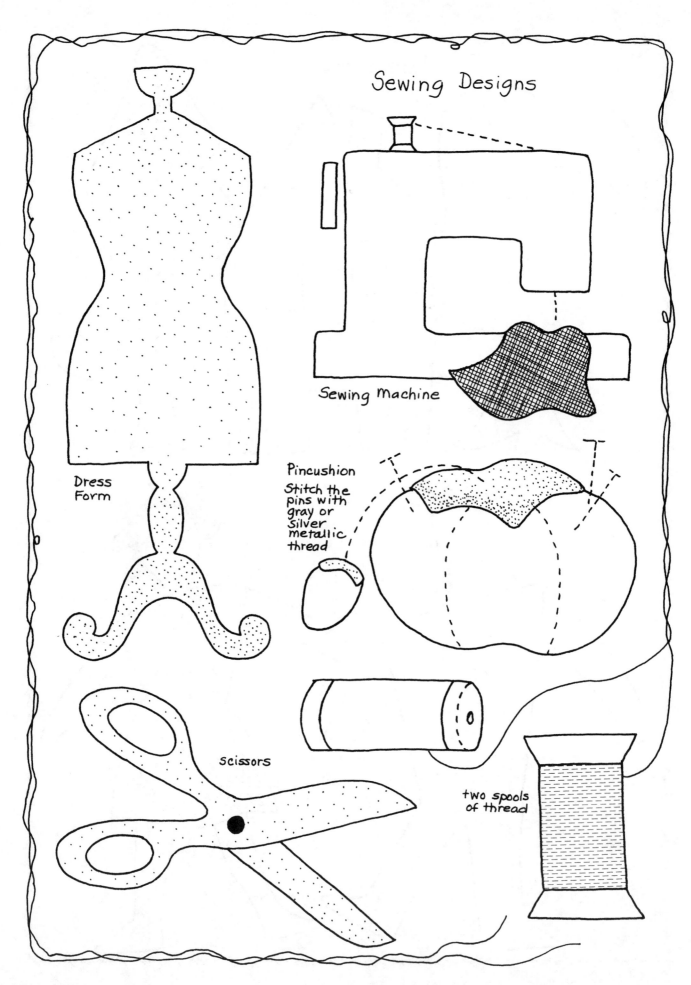

Sewing Designs

Sewing machine

Dress
Form

Pincushion
Stitch the
pins with
gray or
Silver
metallic
thread

Scissors

two spools
of thread

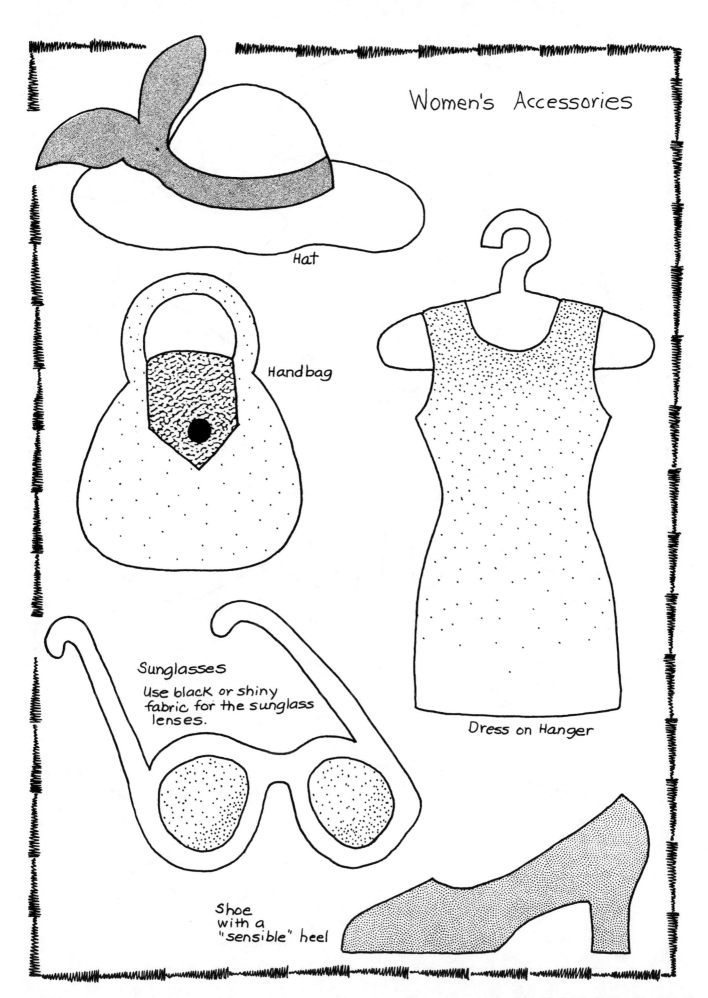

Women's Accessories

Hat

Handbag

Sunglasses
Use black or shiny fabric for the sunglass lenses.

Dress on Hanger

Shoe
with a
"sensible" heel

Underwater Life

Dolphin

Sand Dollar

Starfish

coral

Trout (speckled !)

Fish

Idea:
Use non-fray
fabric for this
fish and cut out
the pieces (eye,
scales, etc.) from
inside the fish so
the background fabric
shows
through.

Fish
Skeleton

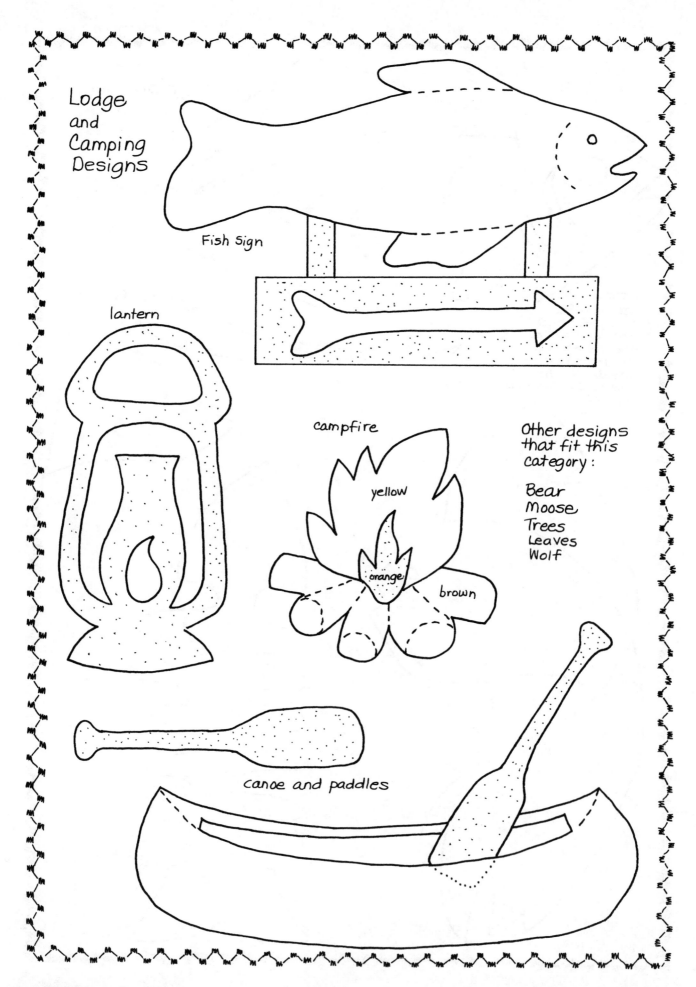

Lodge
and
Camping
Designs

Fish Sign

lantern

campfire

yellow

orange

brown

Other designs
that fit this
category:

Bear
Moose
Trees
Leaves
Wolf

canoe and paddles

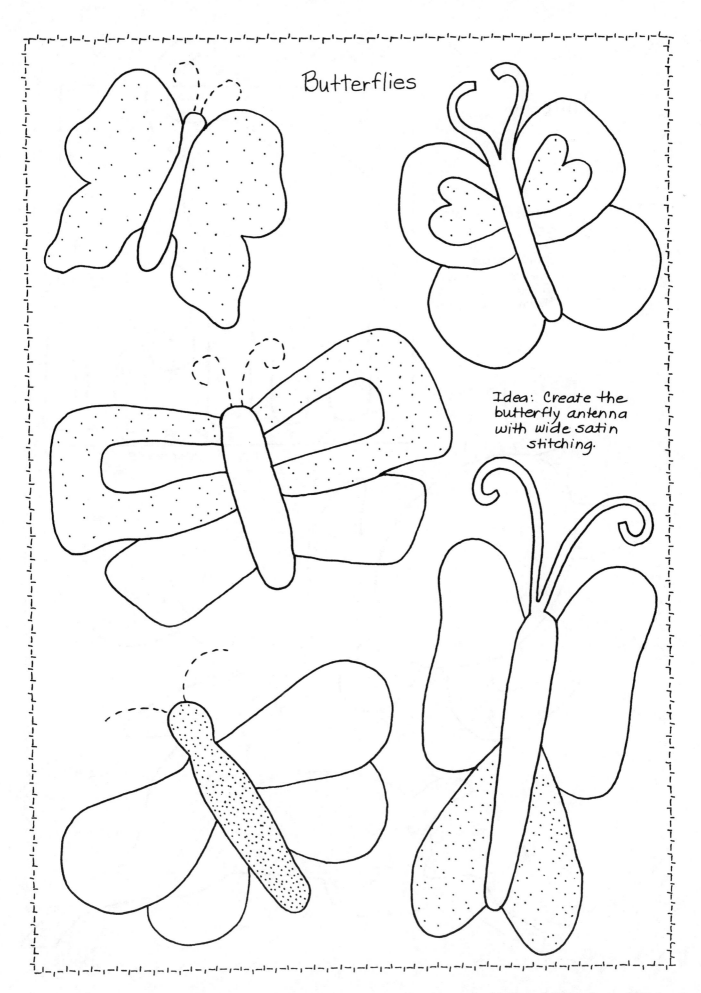

Butterflies

Idea: Create the butterfly antenna with wide satin stitching.

Animals

Mother and baby
elephants are
framed with a
fabric square.
Find more ideas
in the chapter
"Framing Appliques."

elephants

turtle

reindeer

Animals

horse

wolf

moose

bear

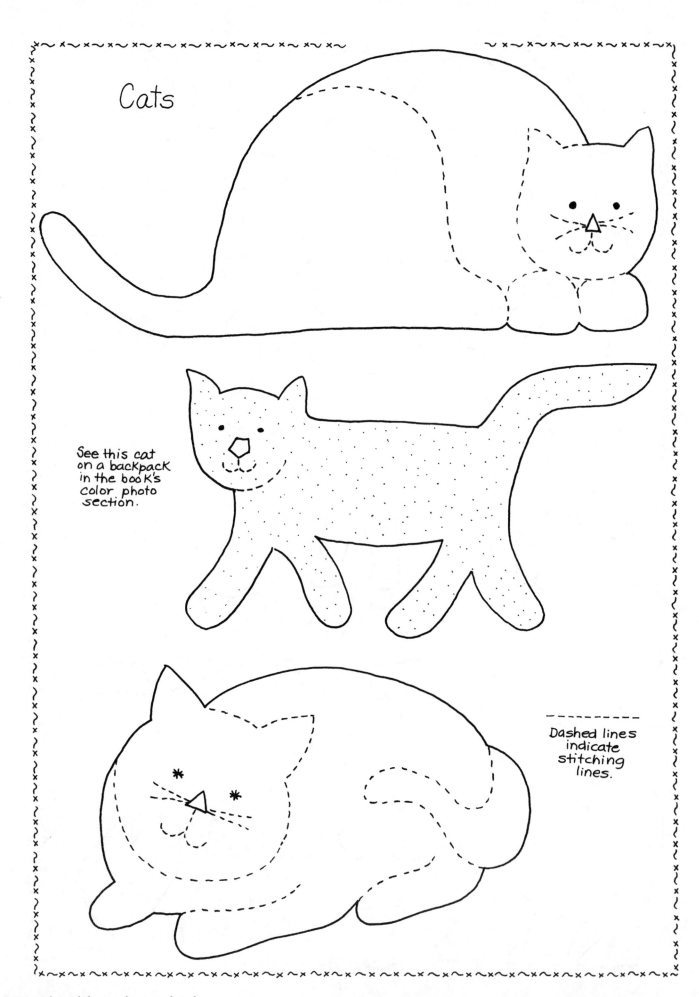

Cats

See this cat on a backpack in the book's color photo section.

Dashed lines indicate stitching lines.

Dogs

dog bone

poodle

paw print

Leaves
and
Branches

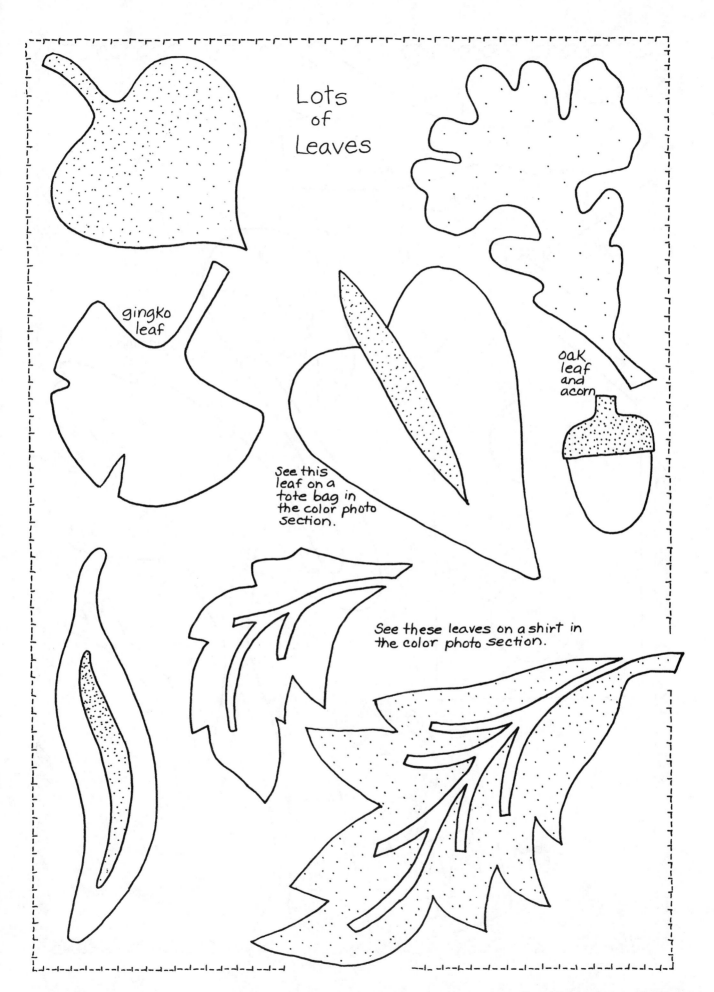

Lots
of
Leaves

gingko
leaf

oak
leaf
and
acorn

See this
leaf on a
tote bag in
the color photo
section.

See these leaves on a shirt in
the color photo section.

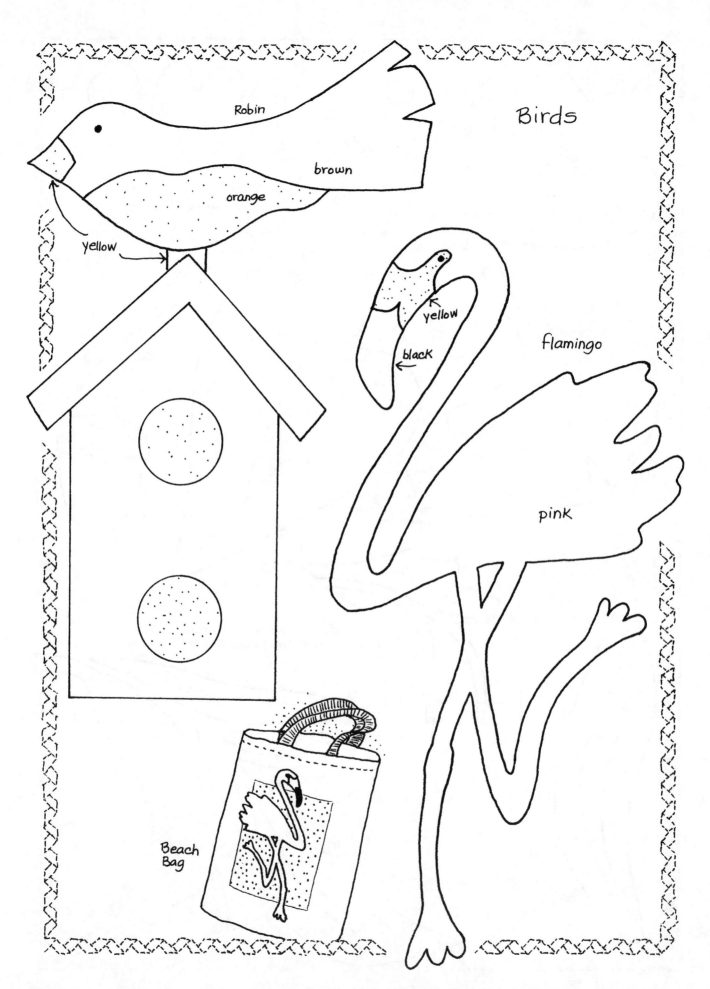

Birds

Robin

brown

orange

yellow

flamingo

yellow

black

pink

Beach Bag

Birds

This page is for margaret.

Idea: Choose a collection of bright and bold colors to make this fantasy bird applique.

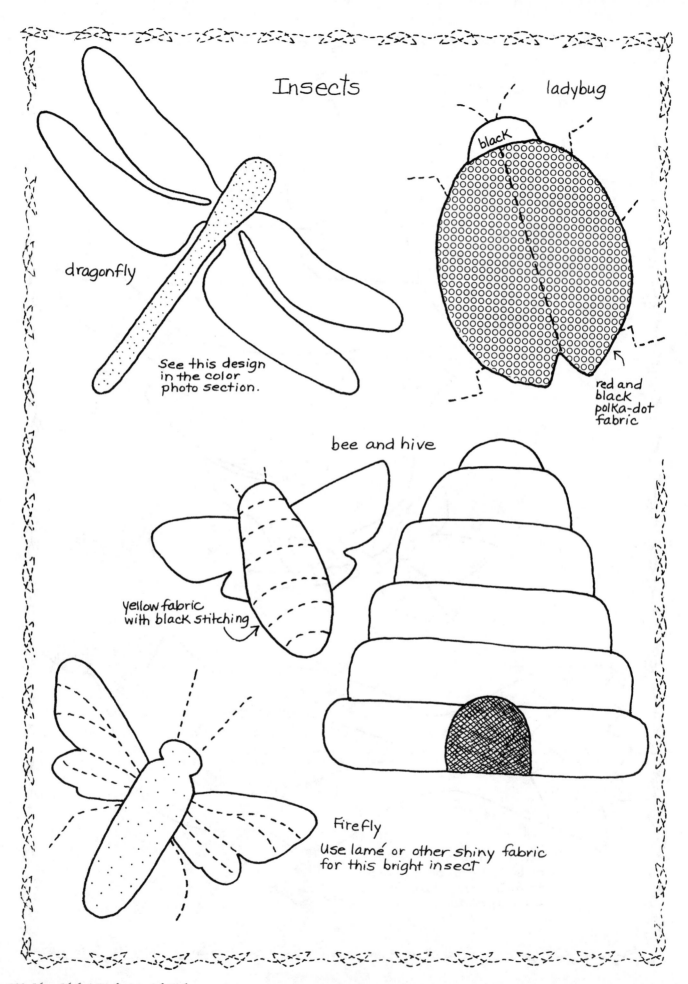

Insects

dragonfly

See this design
in the color
photo section.

ladybug

black

red and
black
polka-dot
fabric

bee and hive

yellow fabric
with black stitching

Firefly

Use lamé or other shiny fabric
for this bright insect

Sports Designs

Cheerleader

Football

ice skate

Basketball Player

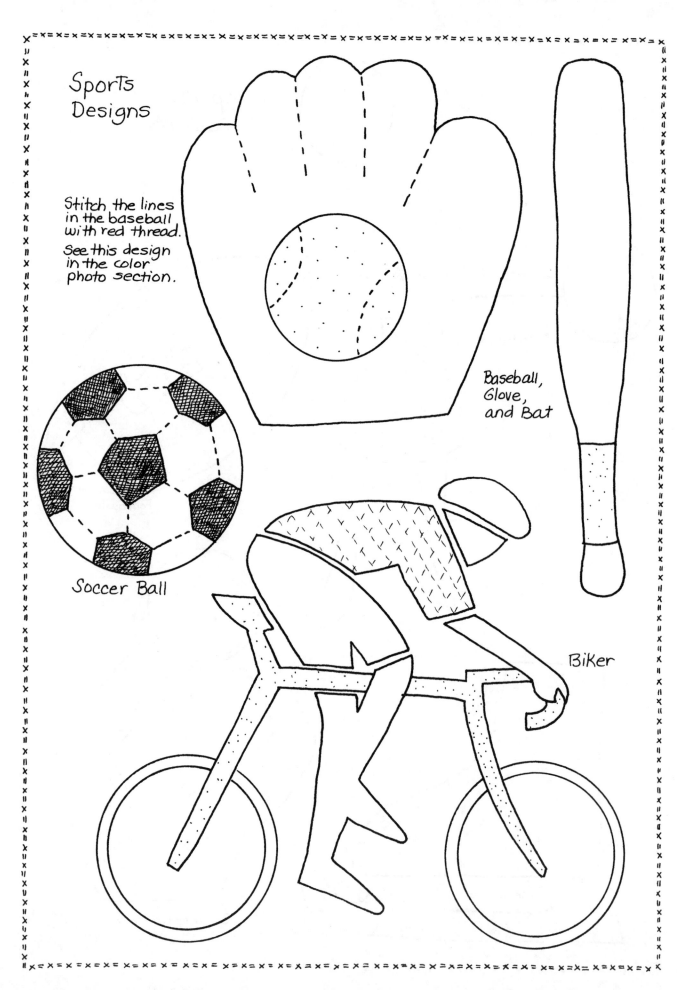

Sports Designs

Stitch the lines in the baseball with red thread.

See this design in the color photo section.

Baseball, Glove, and Bat

Soccer Ball

Biker

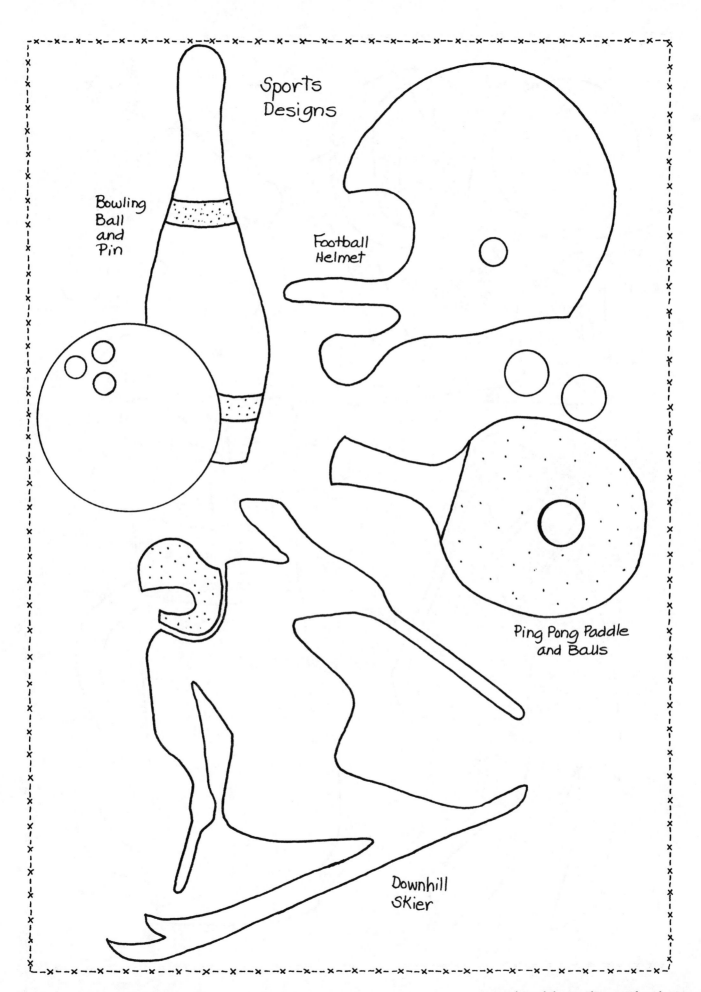

Sports
Designs

Bowling
Ball
and
Pin

Football
Helmet

Ping Pong Paddle
and Balls

Downhill
Skier

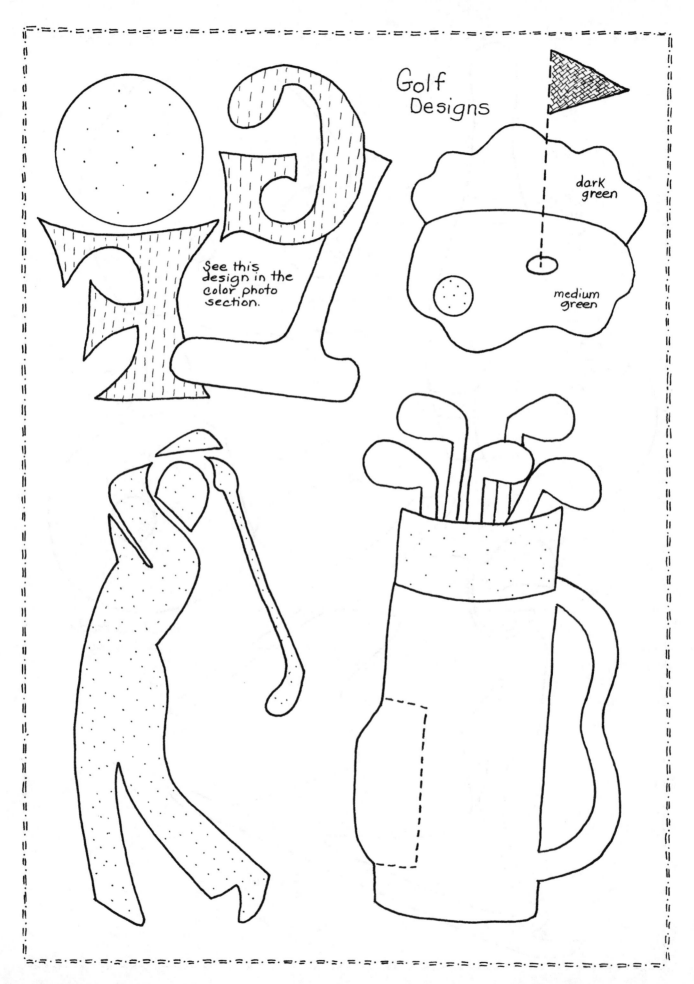

Golf Designs

See this design in the color photo section.

dark green

medium green

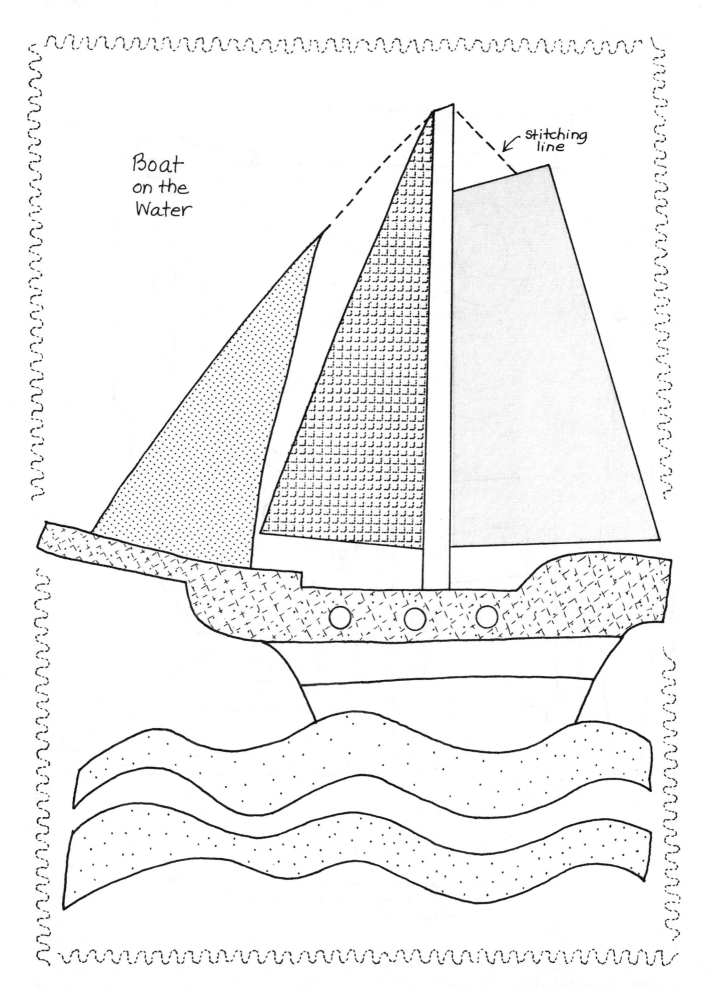

Boat on the Water

stitching line

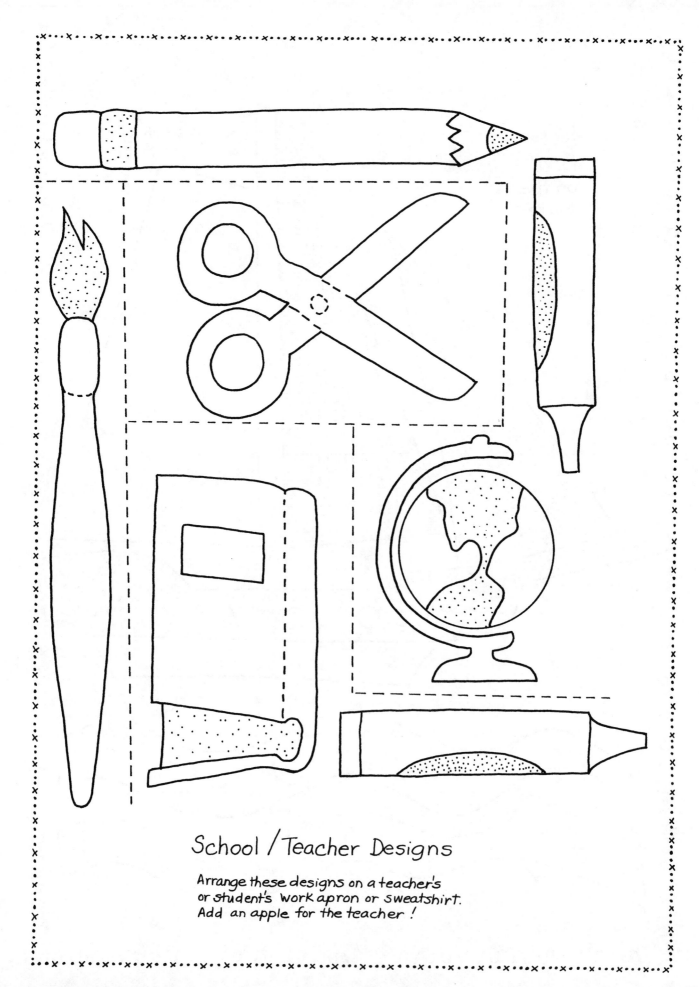

School / Teacher Designs

Arrange these designs on a teacher's
or student's work apron or sweatshirt.
Add an apple for the teacher!

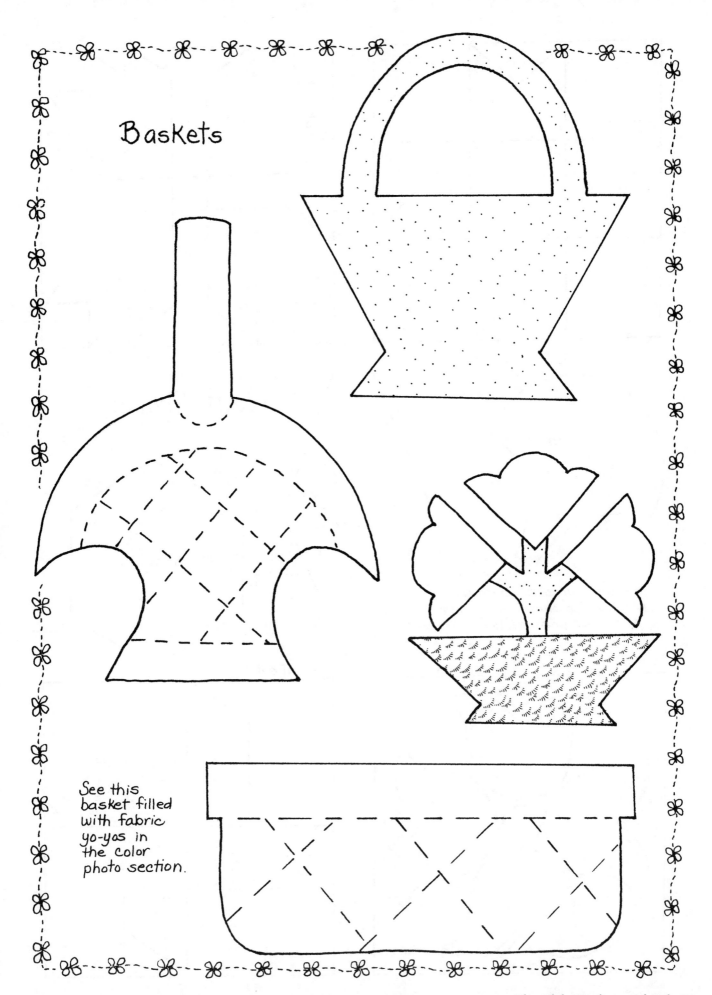

Baskets

See this
basket filled
with fabric
yo-yos in
the color
photo section.

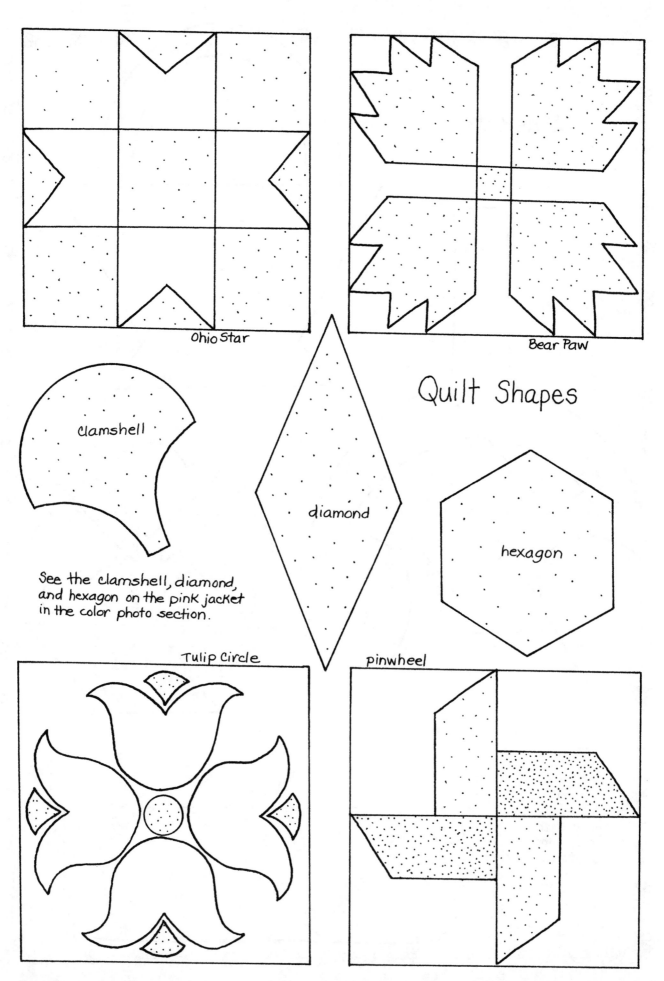

Ohio Star

Bear Paw

Quilt Shapes

Clamshell

diamond

hexagon

See the clamshell, diamond, and hexagon on the pink jacket in the color photo section.

Tulip Circle

pinwheel

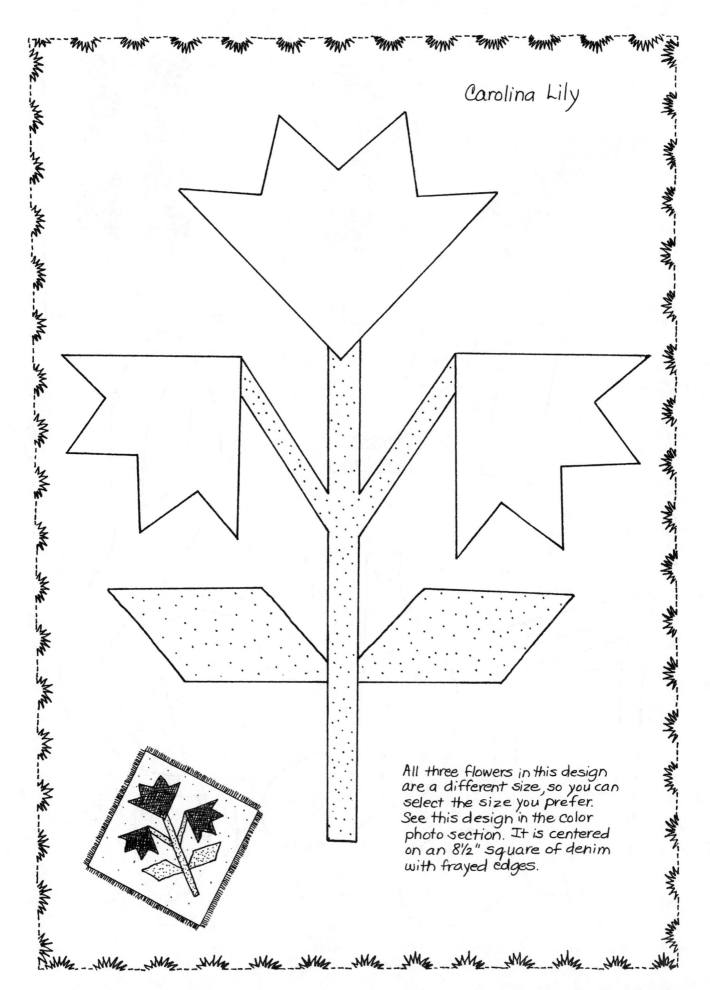

Carolina Lily

All three flowers in this design are a different size, so you can select the size you prefer. See this design in the color photo section. It is centered on an 8½" square of denim with frayed edges.

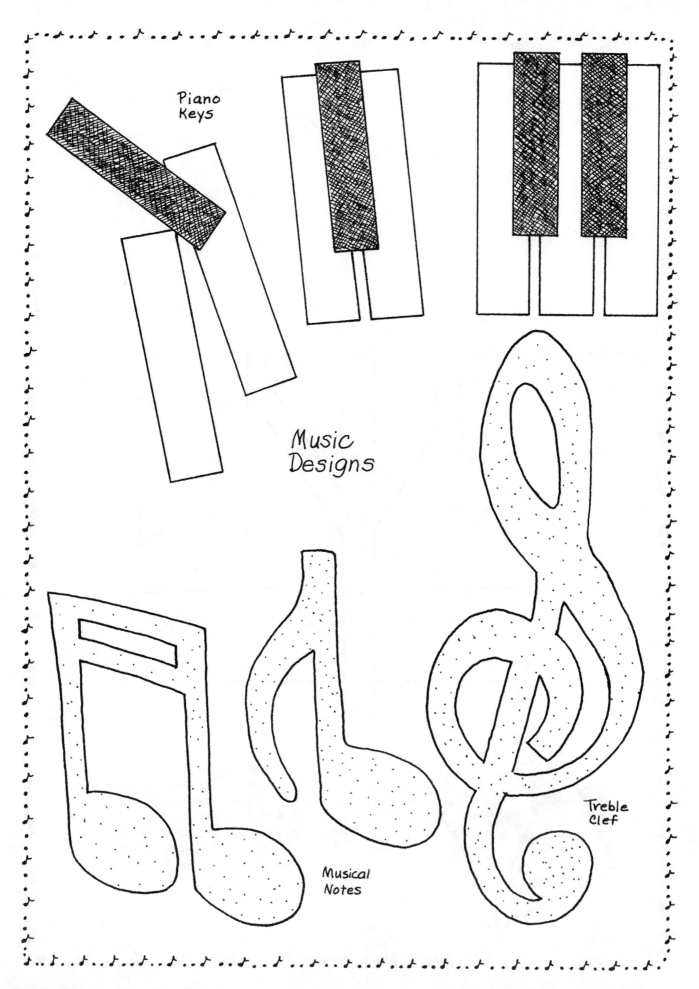

Piano Keys

Music Designs

Musical Notes

Treble Clef

Gardening Designs

Use these designs together as shown
or use them individually.

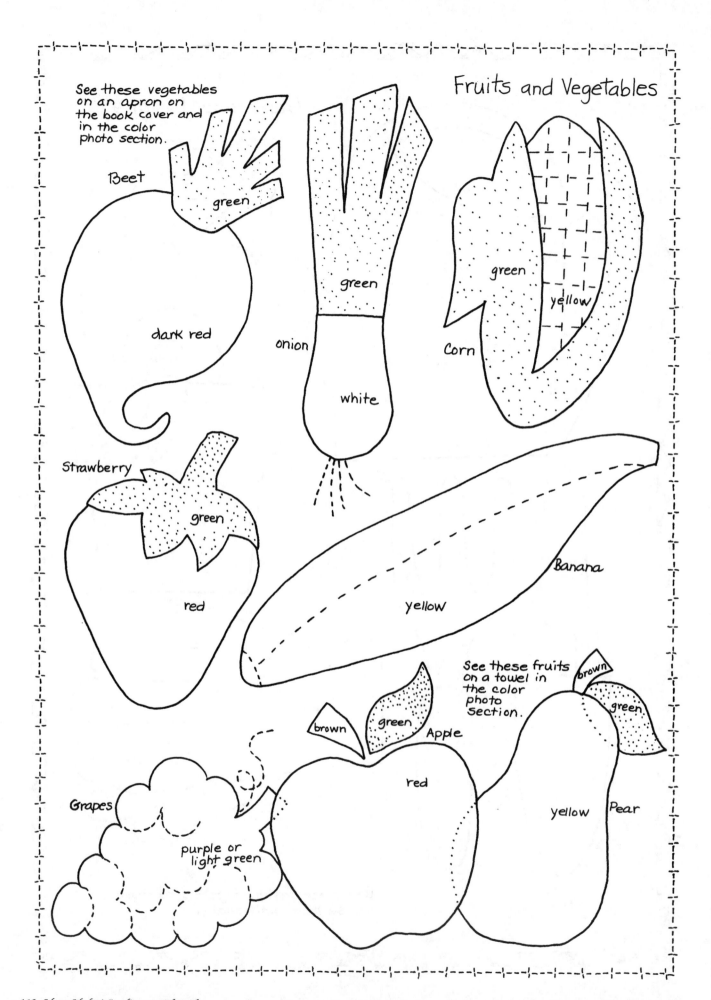

See these vegetables on an apron on the book cover and in the color photo section.

Fruits and Vegetables

Beet

green

dark red

onion

green

white

green

yellow

Corn

Strawberry

green

red

Banana

yellow

See these fruits on a towel in the color photo section.

brown

green

Apple

brown

green

Pear

red

yellow

Grapes

purple or light green

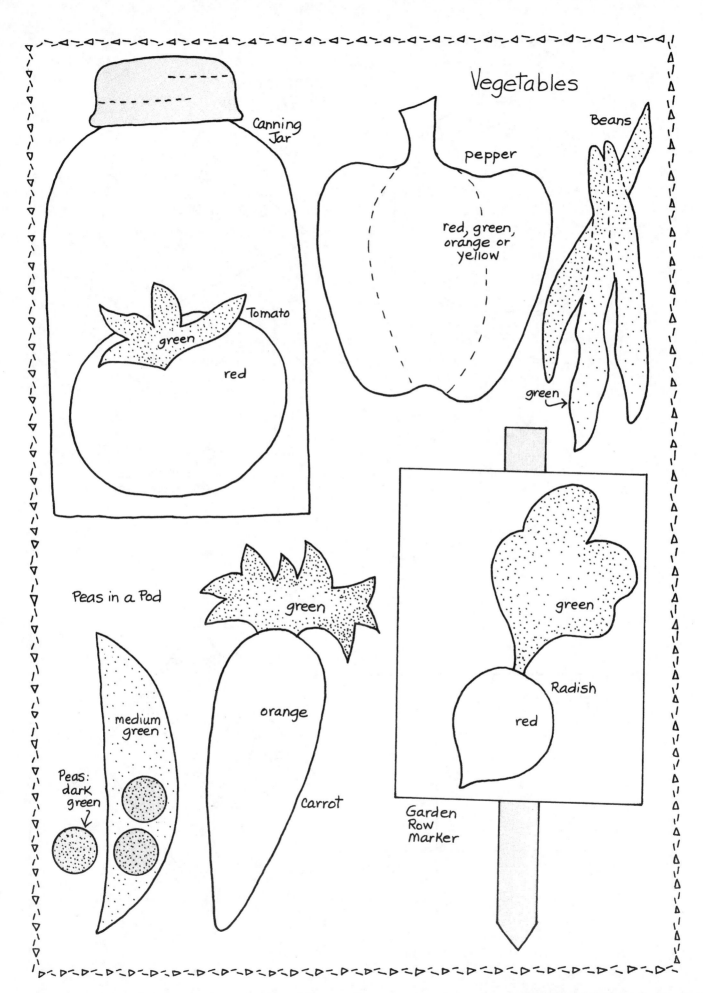

Canning Jar

Vegetables

pepper

Beans

red, green, orange or yellow

green

Tomato

green

red

Peas in a Pod

green

medium green

orange

green

Radish

red

Peas: dark green

Carrot

Garden Row Marker

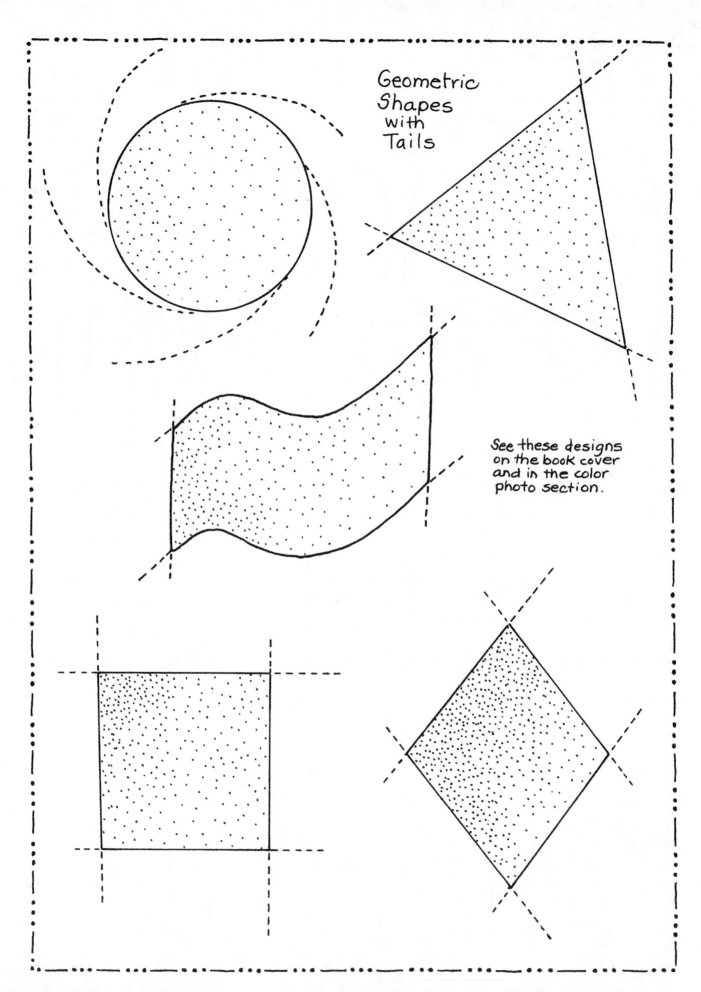

Geometric
Shapes
with
Tails

See these designs
on the book cover
and in the color
photo section.

Overlapping
Diamonds

See this design
in the color
photo section.

For the man's sweatshirt
pictured in the color
photo section, I enlarged
this design on a photo-
copy machine.

Framed Punctuation

Great designs for teachers, students, and e-mail writers

Idea: Cut frames from non-fray fabric. Then cut the punctuation out of the frame so the background fabric will show through the cut out area.

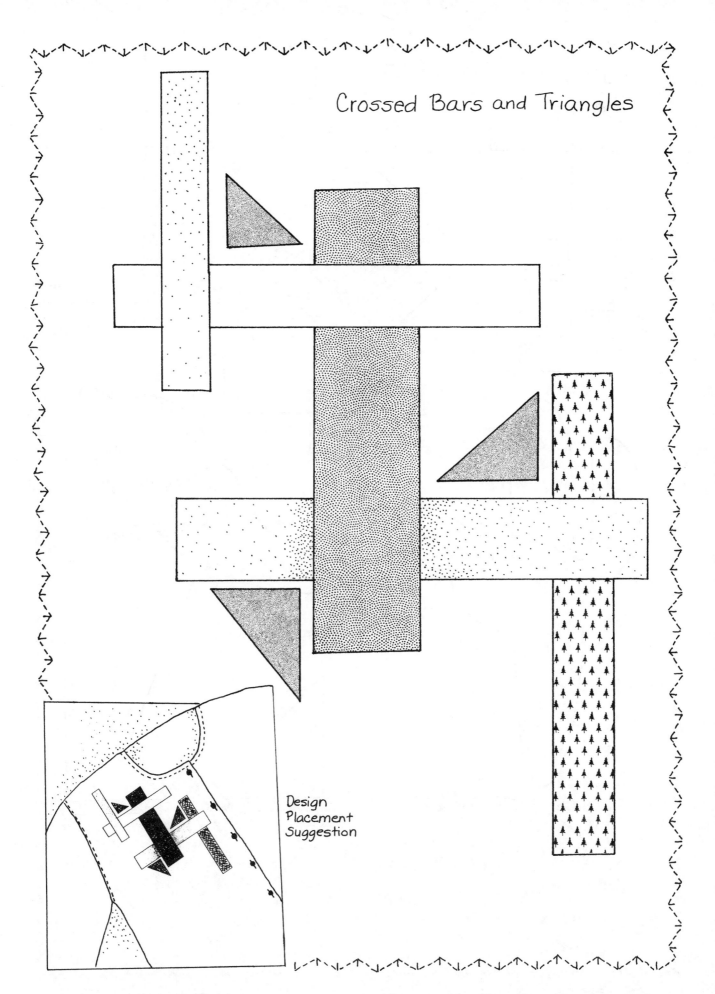

Crossed Bars and Triangles

Design
Placement
Suggestion

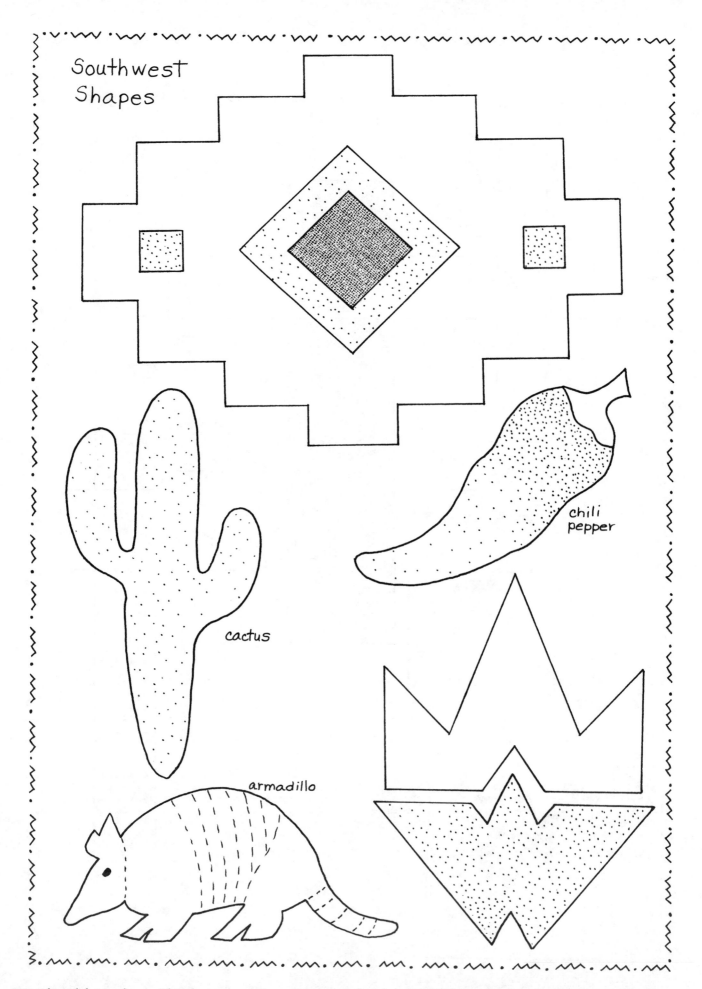

Southwest
Shapes

chili
pepper

cactus

armadillo

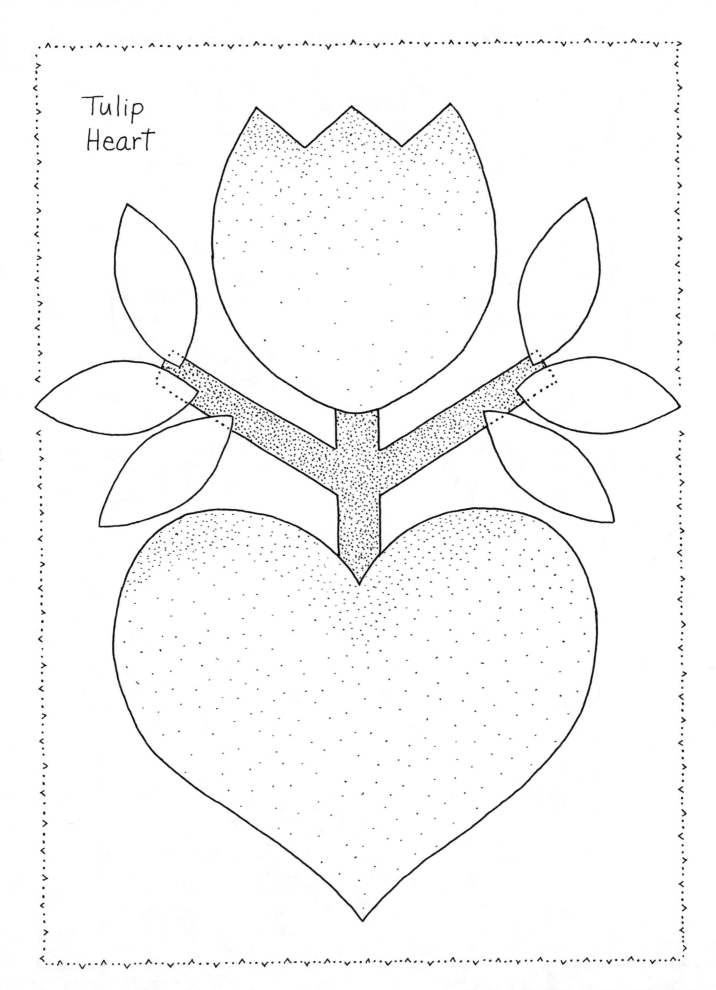

Tulip
Heart

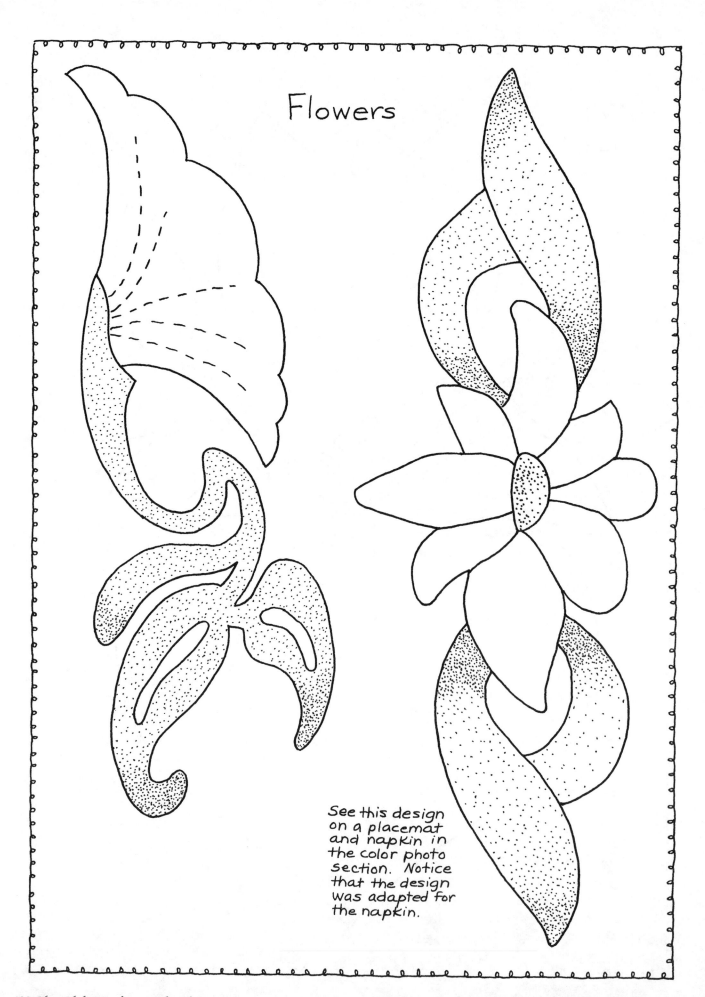

Flowers

See this design
on a placemat
and napkin in
the color photo
section. Notice
that the design
was adapted for
the napkin.

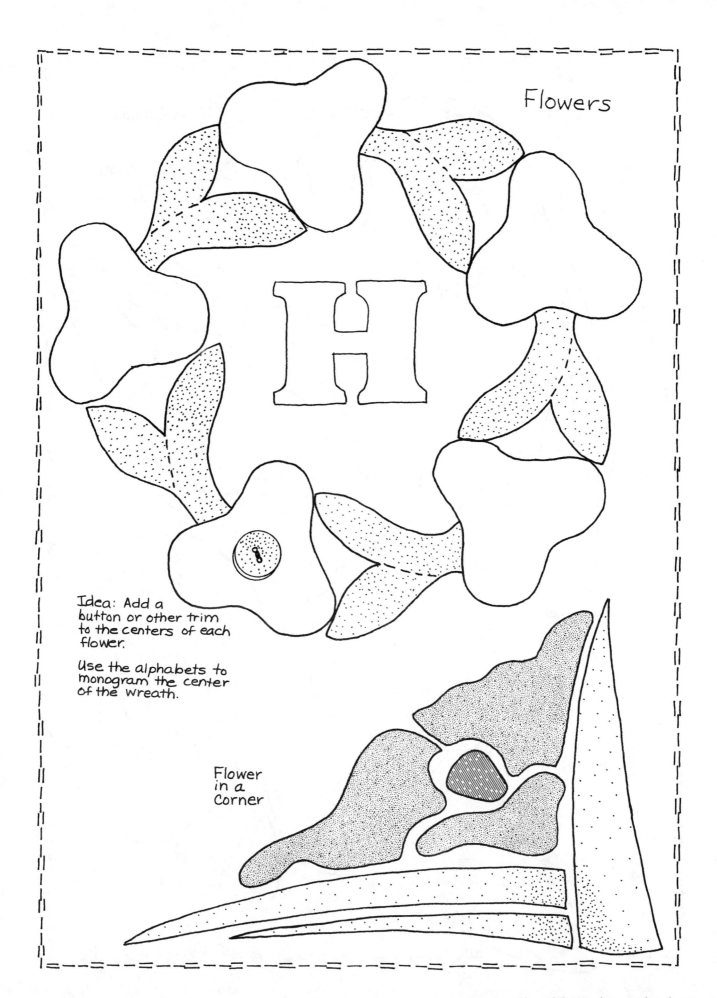

Flowers

Idea: Add a button or other trim to the centers of each flower.

Use the alphabets to monogram the center of the wreath.

Flower in a Corner

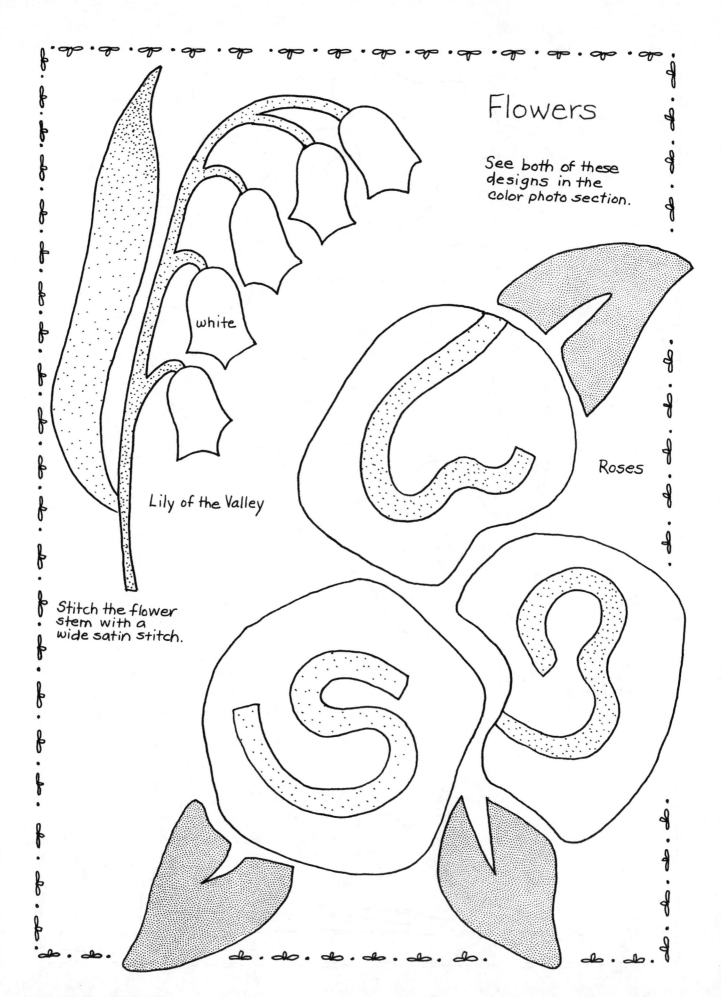

Flowers

See both of these designs in the color photo section.

white

Lily of the Valley

Roses

Stitch the flower stem with a wide satin stitch.

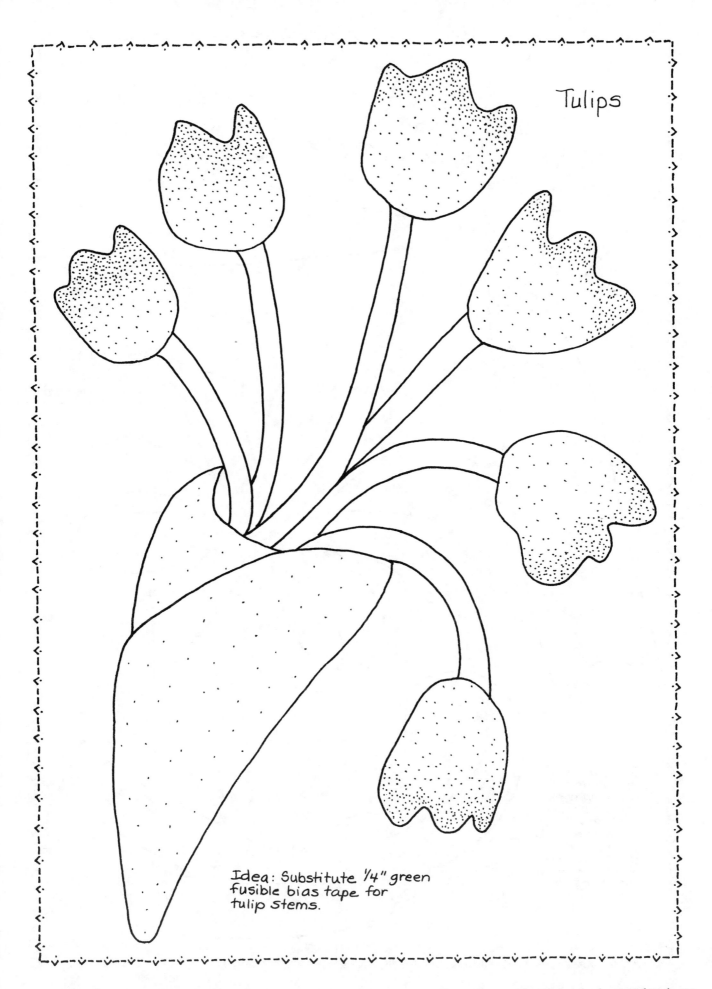

Tulips

Idea: Substitute 1/4" green
fusible bias tape for
tulip stems.

Ribbons

Sew a button in the center of this bow for a dimensional effect.

This page is for my mother, who taught me to tie a sailor's knot, and for my mother-in-law Harriet Mulari who taught me to tie a bow that hangs straight.

Swirls

Hearts

See this design on a gift bag on the book cover and in the color photo section.

Patchwork Heart

See this design on a child's dress in the color photo section.

Hearts

Heart in Hand

Pretzel HearT

Designs for the Seasons

green

yellow

blue

blue

brown

Beach / Summer Scene

Santa Claus with Gift

"Joy" for the December holiday season

Canada Goose – for the fall migratory season
See this design in the color photo section.

white

black

tan

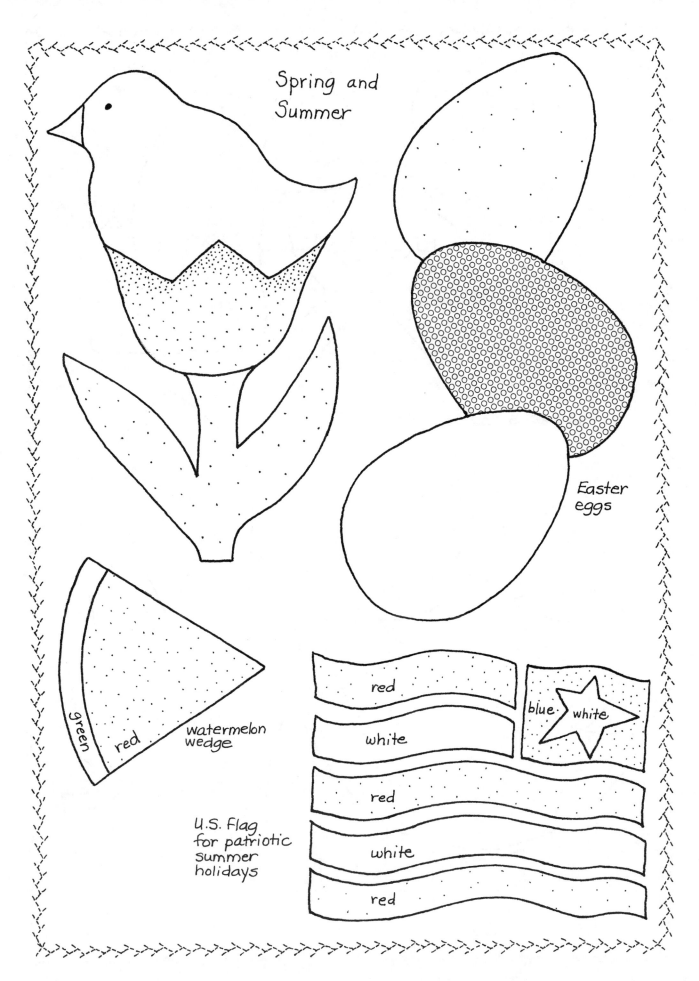

Spring and Summer

Easter eggs

green red watermelon wedge

U.S. flag for patriotic summer holidays

red

white

red

white

red

blue white

Nativity
Scene

Christmas and Winter

Snow Folks

Clothing and Accessories

Hats

Neckwear

neck scarf

vest

Earmuffs

mittens

Shovel

Holly Leaves and Berries in a Frame

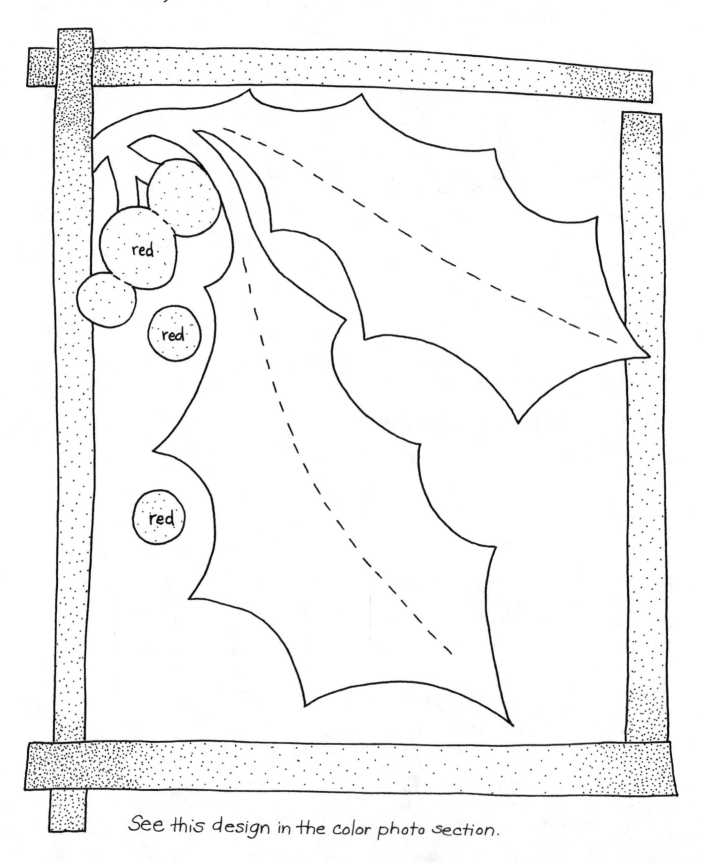

See this design in the color photo section.

Wheat and Pumpkins

For the fall season, add this applique
to a table runner, sweatshirt, or the
back of a denim shirt.

A B C D E
F G H I J
K L M N O
P Q R S
T U V W
X Y Z

A B C D E F
G H I J K L
M N O P Q R
S T U V W
X Y Z 1 2 3
4 5 6 7 8 9 0

Celebration Squares Frame

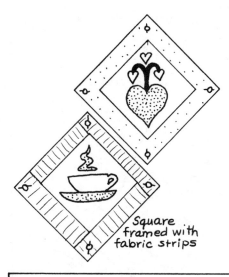

Square framed with fabric strips

For a fun applique project, make Celebration Squares to button "on point" onto garments, tote bags, aprons, or pillows. Move the squares from clothing to accessories when there's a change of season or a holiday.

Use the frame pattern below or make your own frames by sewing 2½" wide fabric strips to the sides of the decorated squares. Cut another piece of fabric for the back of the framed square. Sew right sides together, leaving an opening to turn the square right side out. Sew buttonholes in each corner. You can make the squares reversible by sewing two together instead of using a plain fabric backing for the square.

You will find more ideas with the square applique designs on the following pages.

Buttonhole in each corner

Use this pattern to frame the Celebration Squares designs on the following pages.

Test the frame size first by tracing it from the book and cutting it from paper. Place the pattern "on point" (diamond position, as illustrated above) on a garment or accessory and decide if the frame size is right for your project. Increase or decrease the outer edges and add a seam allowance on all four sides.

The solid lines inside this square form a frame slightly smaller than the design squares on the next pages, so there is an overlap. With frame fabric that ravels, cut a seam allowance inside the frame, as indicated by the dashed lines so you can cut and turn under the fabric to make a neat frame. See the instructions above for cutting and making a back lining for the square.

My favorite framing fabric is Ultrasuede. It does not fray, so you can cut the frame on the solid lines, sew the applique square inside the frame opening, and cut a single line at each corner to make buttonholes without sewing.

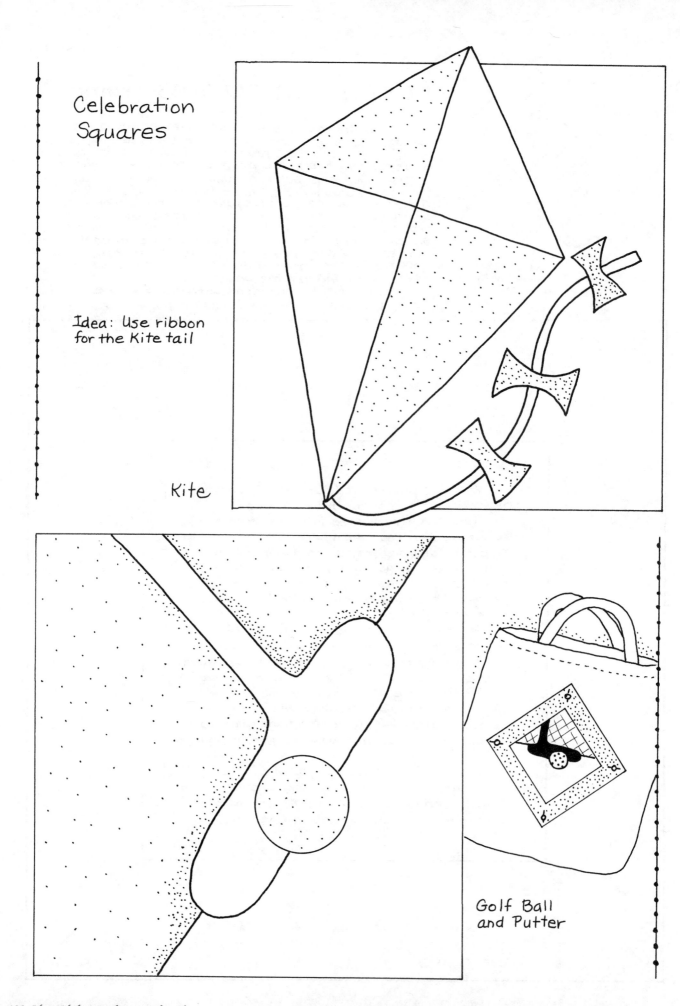

Celebration
Squares

Idea: Use ribbon
for the kite tail

Kite

Golf Ball
and Putter

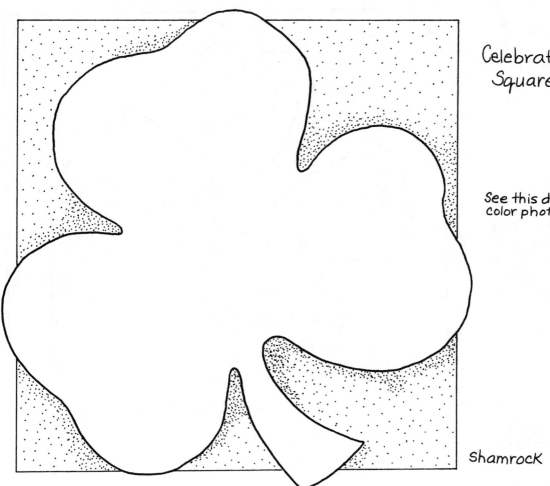

Celebration
Squares

See this design in the
color photo section.

Shamrock

Button Ideas:

Use buttons to trim
the ends of the neck
scarf and the hat
band.

Pin shank buttons
to the garment or
accessory you want
to decorate with
Celebration Squares.
This saves sewing
time and presents
the option of changing
or removing the
buttons. (This
was my best
discovery for
Celebration Squares!)

Snow Woman

Celebration Squares

See additional heart designs in this book as possibilities for Celebration Squares

Hearts

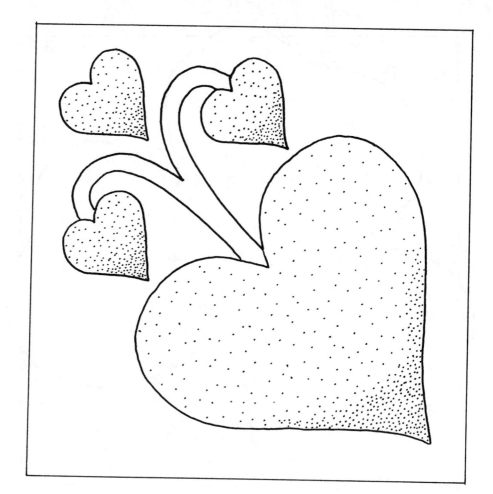

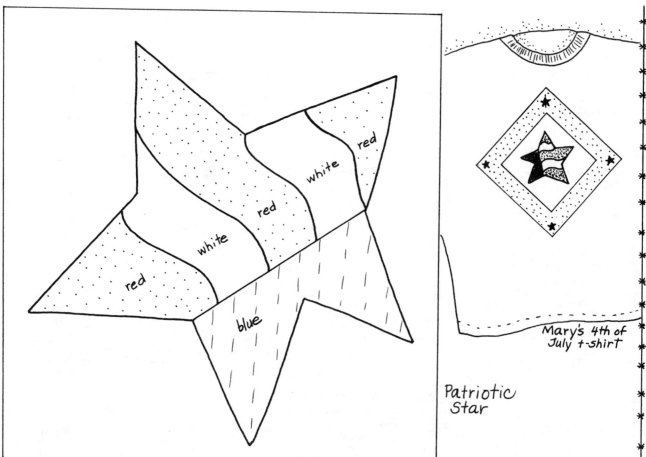

Patriotic Star

Mary's 4th of July t-shirt

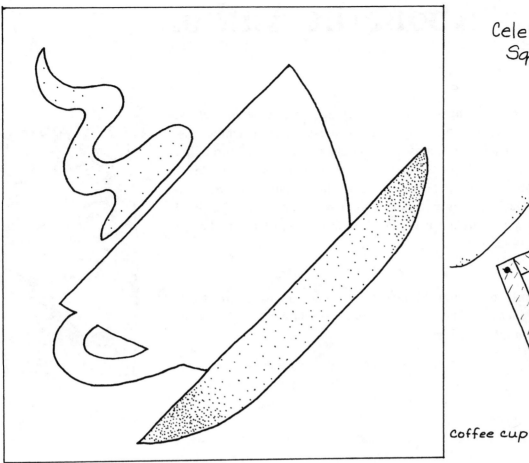

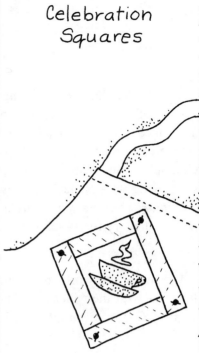

coffee cup

Idea: Use actual
ribbon for trimming
this square.

See this design in
the color photo
section.

Christmas
tree ball

About the Author

Mary Mulari has been writing books and teaching creative sewing classes since 1982. She began by self-publishing *Designer Sweatshirts* and teaching classes in local community education programs. Now her classes are offered throughout the United States and she has written ten books as well as patterns and articles for sewing publications. She appears frequently as a guest on the public television series, "Sewing with Nancy" and on other television sewing programs. Her book, *Mary Mulari's Garments with Style* won the PCM Award of Excellence in the sewing book category for 1995.

Mary lives and works in Aurora, Minnesota. She encourages her readers to contact her with their ideas, observations, and applique stories: Mary's Productions, Box 87-K4, Aurora, MN 55705.

Bibliography

Covert, Anita, Deb Lathrop VanAken, Chelle Dethlefsen, *101 Ideas for Machine Embroidery*, East Lansing, MI. Country Stitches, Ltd., 1997

Drexler, Joyce, *Sulky Secrets to Successful Stabilizing*, Harbor Heights, FL, Sulky of America, 1998.

Garbers, Debbie and Janet F. O'Brien, *Point Well Taken*, Roswell, GA, In Cahoots, 1996.

Hargrave, Harriet. *Mastering Machine Applique*, Lafayette, CA. C & T Publishing, 1991.

Hill, Jane. *The Electric Mola*, Boca Raton, FL, Hillcraft Needle Arts, 1995.

Mulari, Mary. *More Sweatshirts with Style*. Radnor, PA, Chilton Book Co., 1996.

_____. *Sweatshirts with Style*. Radnor, PA, Chilton Book Co., 1993.

_____. *Mary Mulari's Garments with Style*. Radnor, PA, Chilton Book Co., 1995.

Resources for Supplies

Please check locally for fabrics, materials, and equipment mentioned in this book. We need to support our local sewing stores to guarantee they will be there for us when we need their advice, service, enthusiasm, and support.

The following mail order companies are listed to help you find additional sources. If you contact them, please inform them that you read about them in *Mary Mulari Appliques with Style*.

For mail order catalogs of sewing supplies:

Nancy's Notions
P.O. Box 683
Beaver Dam, WI 53916
call 1-800-833-0690 for a free catalog

Clotilde, Inc.
call 1-800-772-2891 for a free catalog

For information about specific products listed in this book, send a **self-addressed stamped envelope** to the following companies.

Bagworks
3933 California Parkway E.
Ft. Worth, TX 76119
blank accessories and garments to trim with appliques

Barrett House
P.O. Box 540585
North Salt Lake City, UT 84054
Wimpole Street Creations
applique embellishments & doilies

Birch Street Clothing Co.
P.O. Box 6901
San Mateo, CA 94403
Swedish black and white tear-away stabilizers

Dragon Threads
410 Canyon Drive N.
Columbus, OH 43214
image transfer paper and project books

LJ Designs
P.O. Box 7542
Reno, NV 89510
water soluble stabilizer paper

Mary's Productions
Box 87-K4
Aurora, MN 55705
Mary Mulari's books and patterns

> **For alphabets, look at the fonts on your computer. By making the letters bold and enlarging them to size 100 or larger, you can print them out and flip over the pages before tracing the letters on paper-backed fusible web.**

Index

Topic Index

Design Index